# Br[illegible]n WILD[illegible]WERS and TREES

## HANDBOOK

First published in 2013 by Miles Kelly Publishing Ltd
Harding's Barn, Bardfield End Green, Thaxted, Essex, CM6 3PX, UK



This edition published in 2019

2 4 6 8 10 9 7 5 3 1

Miles Kelly would like to thank **The Wildlife Trusts** and **The Woodland Trust** for their valuable contributions to this book.

Publishing Director *Belinda Gallagher*
Creative Director *Jo Cowan*
Editorial Director *Rosie Neave*
Editors *Carly Blake, Claire Philip*
Designers *Jo Cowan, Carmen Johnson, Rob Hale*
Cover Design *Joe Jones*
Image Manager *Liberty Newton*
Production *Elizabeth Collins, Jennifer Brunwin-Jones*
Reprographics *Stephan Davis, Thom Allaway, Jennifer Cozens*
Woodland Trust Advisor *Graham Blight*
The Wildlife Trusts Advisors *Adam Cormack, Mary Porter*
Assets *Lorraine King*

ISBN 978-1-78617-667-7

Printed in China

British Library Cataloguing-in-Publication Data
A catalogue record for this book is available from the British Library

## ACKNOWLEDGEMENTS

The publishers would like to thank the following artists who have contributed to this book:
Bridgette James, Mike Foster, Andrea Morandi, Mike Saunders, Vivien Wilson

The publishers would like to thank the following sources for the use of their photographs:

**Colin Varndell** 19(l); 25(r); 35(r); 37(r); 39(r); 43(r); 73(r); 79(r); 87(r); 91(r); 95(r) **Dreamstime.com** 122(cr) Ryszard Laskowski; 126 Elena Elisseeva; 146 Griffin024; 164 Ivonne Wierink; 192 Pavel Kalouš; 212 Ryszard Laskowski; 220 Marco Regalia **FLPA** 122 B. Borrell Casals; 26 Nigel Cattline; 38 Tony Hamblin; 48 G E Hyde; 60 Tony Wharton; 62 Tony Hamblin; 66 Richard Becker; 70 Robert Canis; 72 Robert Canis; 73(c) Roger Wilmshurst; 78 Tony Wharton; 82 Gary K Smith; 90 Roger Wilmshurst; 92 Richard Becker; 94 Martin B Withers; 98 John Hawkins; 100 Nigel Cattlin; 104 Martin Woike/Nis/Minden Pictures; 108 Joke Stuurman/Nis/Minden Pictures; 110 John Hawkins; 112 Robert Canis; 134 FotoNatura/FN/Minden; 136 Tony Wharton; 144 Richard Becker; 172 Erica Olsen; 184 Martin H Smith; 190 Peter Entwistle; 198 Tony Wharton; 210 Gary K Smith; 216 Tony Hamblin; 222 Bob Gibbons **Fotolia.com** Cover(back, c) Oleg Belyakov; 18 Gail Johnson; 19(r) AndreyTTL; 20 AndreyTTL; 34 Bill; 40 Sergey; 51(c) RobynMac; 83(c) Olena Kucherenko; 116–117 (bg) Oleg Belyakov; 124 Freddy Smeets; 160 Jgz; 174 Oleg Belyakov; 200 Eric Weight; 218 Martina Berg **Getty** 30 Scenics and Science/Oxford Scientific **iStock** 12(cl) fotohorst, redmal; 24 istock; 28 Enfys; 32 Andrew_Howe; 42 brightstorm; 50 hmproudlove; 52 rsaulyte; 54 AlbyDeTweede; 56 Andrew_Howe; 58 Rob_Ellis; 64 4dings; 68 Argument; 76 Andrew_Howe; 80 vchernian; 84 tomazl; 86 Andrew_Howe; 88 iStock; 102 Andrew_HoweJo Brewer: 156; 176 **Mike Alsford** 10 **NHPA** 16 Martin Garwood; 36 Stephen Dalton; 140 Dr Eckart Pott; 180 Stephen Dalton **Nature Picture Library** Cover(front) Michael Hutchinson **Philip Wells** 158 **Shutterstock.com** Cover(back, r) Ivan M Munoz; 1 Madlen; 3 Regien Paassen; 6–7 Ivan M Munoz; 40 Targn Pleiades; 44 stoupa; 106 Cristian Mihai; 120 Creative Travel Projects; 130 Marek Mierzejewski; 138 Douglas Freer; 186 Olga Nikonova **The Wildlife Trusts** 120 (cr) The Wildlife Trusts; 132 Neil Aldridge; 142 Rachel Scopes; 148 Neil Aldridge; 150 Erica tetralix; 162 Les Binns; 170 Les Binns; 178 Philip Precey; 182 Philip Precey; 188 Eddie Asbery; 204 Dave Appleton; 214 Adam Cormack **WTPL** 13(r), (l); 15 **WTPL/Pete Holmes** 11(br), (cbl), (ctr), 11(tl)

All other images are from the Miles Kelly Archives

Every effort has been made to acknowledge the source and copyright holder of each picture. Miles Kelly Publishing apologizes for any unintentional errors or omissions.

THE wildlife TRUSTS

WOODLAND TRUST

www.mileskelly.net

# British WILDFLOWERS and TREES HANDBOOK

Written by:

Miles Kelly

# Contents

## TREES


Introducing Trees 8
Seasonwatch 9
Wonderful woodlands 10
How to measure trees 11
How to plant a tree 12
How to use 14

### OVAL

- O Alder 16
- O Aspen 18
- O Beech 20
- O Black poplar 22
- O Blackthorn 24
- O Box 26
- O Buckthorn 28
- O Common lime 30
- O Crab apple 32
- O Dogwood 34
- O English elm 36
- O Goat willow 38
- O Hazel 40
- O Hornbeam 42
- O Mulberry 44
- O Pear 46
- O Plum 48
- O Silver birch 50
- O Wayfaring tree 52
- O Whitebeam 54
- O Wild cherry 56
- O Wild privet 58
- O Wych elm 60

### LONG

- O Holly 62
- O Magnolia 64
- O Pedunculate oak 66
- O Sea buckthorn 68
- O Sessile oak 70
- O Spindle 72
- O Sweet chestnut 74
- O White willow 76

### HAND-SHAPED

- O Field maple 78
- O Guelder rose 80
- O Hawthorn 82
- O Horse chestnut 84
- O London plane 86
- O Sycamore 88
- O Wild service tree 90

### COMPOUND

- O Ash 92
- O Elder 94
- O Laburnum 96
- O Rowan 98
- O Walnut 100

### NEEDLE

- O Cedar of Lebanon 102
- O European larch 104
- O Giant sequoia 106
- O Juniper 108
- O Norway spruce 110
- O Scots pine 112
- O Yew 114

# WILDFLOWERS


Introducing Wildflowers 118
What is a flower? 119
About Wildlife Watch 120
Become a wildflower detective 121
How to use 122

## WHITE

- O Bindweed 124
- O Chamomile 126
- O Daisy 128
- O Garlic mustard 130
- O Meadowsweet 132
- O Oxeye daisy 134
- O Sea kale 136
- O Snowdrop 138
- O Water-plantain 140
- O Wood anemone 142

## GREEN

- O Broad-leaved helleborine 144
- O Lords and ladies 146

## PINK

- O Bee orchid 148
- O Cross-leaved heath 150
- O Deptford pink 152
- O Foxglove 154
- O Great willowherb 156
- O Heather 158
- O Herb-robert 160
- O Indian balsam 162
- O Purple loosestrife 164
- O Red campion 166
- O Thrift 168

## RED & ORANGE

- O Marsh cinquefoil 170
- O Pheasant's eye 172
- O Poppy 174
- O Scarlet pimpernel 176

## BLUE & PURPLE

- O Bluebell 178
- O Brooklime 180
- O Bugle 182
- O Butterwort 184
- O Columbine 186
- O Cornflower 188
- O Devil's-bit scabious 190
- O Harebell 192
- O Marsh violet 194
- O Meadow cranesbill 196
- O Sea pea 198
- O Teasel 200
- O Tufted vetch 202

## YELLOW

- O Cowslip 204
- O Dandelion 206
- O Flax-leaved St John's wort 208
- O Lesser celandine 210
- O Marsh marigold 212
- O Primrose 214
- O Silverweed 216
- O Sunflower 218
- O Yellow iris 220
- O Yellow rattle 222

Glossary 224


**Checklist:** Mark off your tree and wildflower sightings in the tick boxes.

# TREES

# Introducing Trees

*We owe a lot to trees. They warm us, shelter us and provide us with building materials. If it wasn't for trees, this book wouldn't be printed on paper and you wouldn't be reading it!*

*The least we can do in return is get to know their names. Knowing what tree you are leaning against or standing under will give you an amazing insight into what's going on all around you. Being able to identify a tree means you can have a good guess at what species of butterfly and moth caterpillars may be chewing through its leaves, which birds may be nesting in its boughs and what fungi might burst through the leaf litter come the autumn.*

*But where to start? Well – you have already made the first step in tree identification by holding this book! Here, there are fifty fantastic tree species to discover, including those you may already recognise.*

*In this section you will find each species clearly presented. Use the images of the leaf, twig and tree shape to help with identification. Find essential information in the factfile, and use the photofile to discover what wildlife you might see living in or near the tree. Make sure to take notes and record your sightings and activities.*

*Most importantly, enjoy learning about these fascinating and important plants!*

Nick Baker

# Seasonwatch

Get up close to nature all year round with the Woodland Trust's nature detectives CLUB. Each season brings plenty of changes and events, from spring bluebells to juicy summer blackberries.

**Spring:** Look out for signs of the natural world bursting into life – discover blossoms on trees and hedges, identify new leaves emerging from buds and hunt for minibeasts.

explore a bluebell wood in spring

discover wildflowers in summer

**Summer:** Make the most of the year's longest days – have a picnic in the shade of a tree in full leaf, identify butterflies collecting nectar from flowers, sail a leaf boat down a stream, and capture a colourful wildflower meadow on camera.

play conkers in autumn

**Autumn:** Enjoy nature's dazzling autumn display – scrunch through colourful, fallen leaves, collect juicy blackberries to turn into tasty treats, plant an acorn and make a house for a hedgehog to hibernate in.

plant a tree in winter

**Winter:** Wrap up warm in these colder months and splash through puddles on a welly wander in the woods. You can also make a bird feeder and identify animal prints in the snow or mud.

Woodland Trust
**nature**detectives
**CLUB**

Join the Woodland Trust's nature detectives CLUB to enjoy year-round family fun outdoors, with ideas and activities every week to make the most of each season. Club members get a fantastic wall chart with stickers and seasonal packs.

**www.naturedetectives.org.uk/365**

# Wonderful woodlands

## www.VisitWoods.org.uk

If you like nature and outdoor adventures, the Woodland Trust's website VisitWoods.org.uk is a great place to discover amazing woodlands close to home, and all over the country.

### Plan your visit

You can find your nearest wood with a simple postcode or town name search. There are over 10,000 woods on the database, so there's plenty to choose from.

### Get exploring

VisitWoods.org.uk are always coming up with loads of new ideas for things to do in the woods. On the website you can download stuff to help you spot wildlife, go on a woodland scavenger hunt, build a cool den and even create your own tree sculpture.

### Take part

The website is interactive, meaning you can share your wildlife sightings by uploading photos and recording your stories to document your adventures.

Log on today to start your woodland adventure!

WOODLAND TRUST

VisitWoods.org.uk

# How to measure trees

Here are two easy, fun and safe ways to measures trees. For species that can live to an ancient age, measure the girth of the trunk. For species that are more short-lived, you can try measuring the height instead.

Once you have taken your measurements, remember to tick the 'Measured it!' stamp.

## Measure the girth

**You will need:**

If you have one, take a measuring tape, but if you don't, you can estimate the girth of the tree by hugging it!

**Measuring tape** Measure around the trunk at 1.5 metres from the ground. If you can't measure the tree at this height then make a note of the height at which you measured the girth.

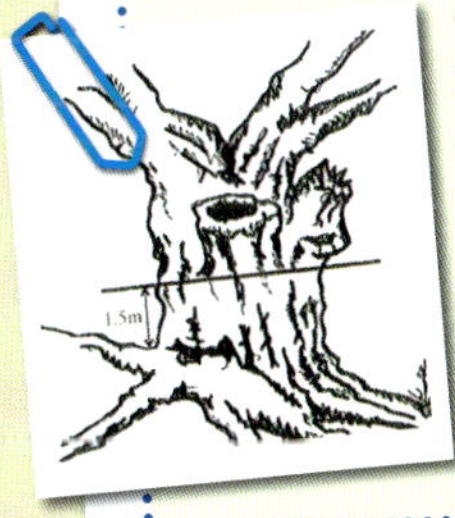


**Hugging** A standard British hug (fingertip to fingertip) is 1.5 m long. With some friends, wrap your arms around the trunk so that your fingertips touch each others' fingertips. Each person around the tree equals one 'hug'.

If you can, work out exactly where the tree is on a map. Take some photos of the tree.

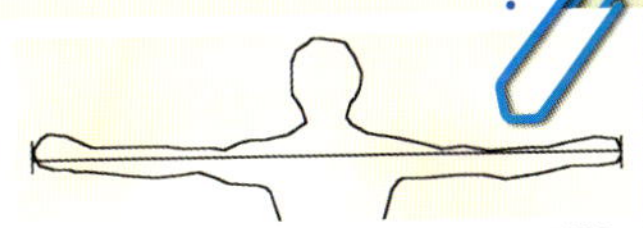

1.5 METRES: ONE BRITISH STANDARD HUG

## Measure the height

**You will need:**

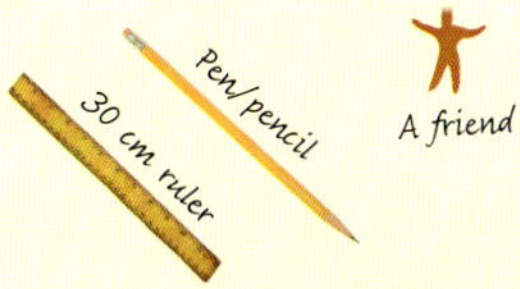


1 Ask a friend to stand next to the tree.

2 Facing the tree, hold your ruler upright and at arms length. Walk away from the tree until it 'fits' on the ruler.

3 According to the ruler, record how tall your friend is and how tall the tree is. Work out how many times your friend goes nto the height of the tree.

4 Multiply this number by your friend's actual height (in metres) and this will give you the rough height of the tree.

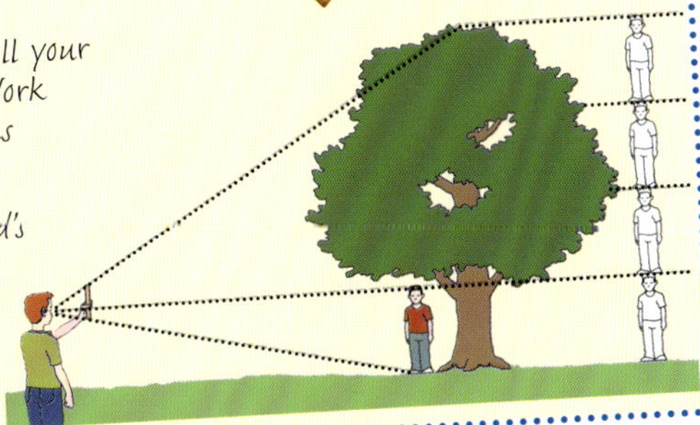

# How to plant a tree

Planting trees is great for the environment and easier than you might think. Choose a native tree and the benefits are even greater as these provide food and shelter for our wildlife.

## Planting your tree from a seed

Try planting a tree from seeds you have collected yourself. You can collect seeds from late summer to autumn, once they have started dropping from trees.

### Collecting and preparing

**Cones** Let cones dry out naturally and they will release their seeds.

**Fleshy fruits** Remove all flesh from seeds, such as cherries, berries and apples, and put in water. Only use the seeds that sink.

**Nuts** De-shell nuts, such as acorns and conkers, and put in water. Keep the nuts that sink.

**Winged seeds** Break in half to separate pairs. These can be planted with wings on.

### Planting

1 All of the these seeds can be planted immediately in a container. Use small plant pots, old milk cartons or yogurt pots. Make holes in the bottom for drainage.

2 Fill containers with a mix of peat-free compost and sand. Sow alder, birch or pine seeds on top then cover with a thin layer of compost. Acorns and nuts should be sown about 5 cm deep. Press down the compost.

3 You can leave the pots outside over autumn and winter. Put them in a shady spot against a wall and cover with mesh to protect from birds and mice.

4 Once your seeds have germinated in spring, keep them well watered. When your seedlings are 20 to 40 cm tall they are ready to plant out (see next page for details).

### TOP TREE-PLANTING TIPS

- If you have a small garden, avoid willow and poplar. Try hawthorn, hazel, holly, rowan, crab apple or box.
- If you have a large, spacious garden, try oak, ash, beech, Scots pine or yew.
- Make sure there is enough room for your tree to grow – don't plant it too close to buildings or pipes.
- If you are planting more than one tree, leave 2 m between them.

# Planting your tree from a sapling

An easy way to plant a tree is from a sapling (partly grown tree). You can buy saplings from your local garden centre, or online at www.woodlandtrustshop.com/trees

1 Give the roots of your sapling a good soak in a bucket of water before you plant them.

2 Carefully remove the sapling from its container. Check it for damage and remove any broken roots.

3 Decide on your planting spot. Dig a hole twice as wide and slightly deeper than the sapling roots. Save the turf for later.

4 You may need to make the hole bigger to avoid bending the roots – try your sapling in the hole to check.

5 Place your sapling upright in the hole. Break up the dug-out soil and fill in carefully but firmly around the roots.

6 Tread down the soil firmly and add some more soil if needed. Tread down again.

7 Take the pieces of turf saved from earlier and place them upside down around your sapling and press them down.

8 Finally, 'heel in' the earth around the tree. Give your sapling a gentle tug – it should be firmly in place.

9 Tidy up and apply mulch (material laid down to keep in moisture) around the base of your sapling.

10 Start your tree diary by writing regular notes on your tree's progress.

## LOOKING AFTER YOUR TREE

Now that you have planted your tree, you need to look after it:

- Keep a one-metre circle around the base free from grass and plants for the first year.
- Add some mulch around the base. Bark mulch is best, but newspaper or grass clippings are better than nothing! Mulch provides nutrients to the tree and keeps in moisture.
- Check the tree regularly. 'Heel it in' (press firmly round the base with your heel) if it's rocked in the wind.
- Small trees planted in the winter shouldn't need watering, but larger trees may need watering through the first year and during dry spells.

For more information visit: www.woodlandtrust.org.uk/communitytrees

# How to use

*Use this guide to help you find your way around the tree section. Read information about 50 different species of trees, including vital statistics, wildlife you might see near the tree, detailed illustrations and simple identification tips.*

**Photofile**
If you spot the bug, bird or fungus featured for each tree, tick the 'Seen it!' stamp.

**My notes**
Make notes about your tree sightings.

**Measure**
If you measure the girth or the height of the tree tick the 'Measured it!' stamp.

**My drawings and photos**
Fill these spaces with your sketches and photographs, and stick in a leaf or photo of the tree.

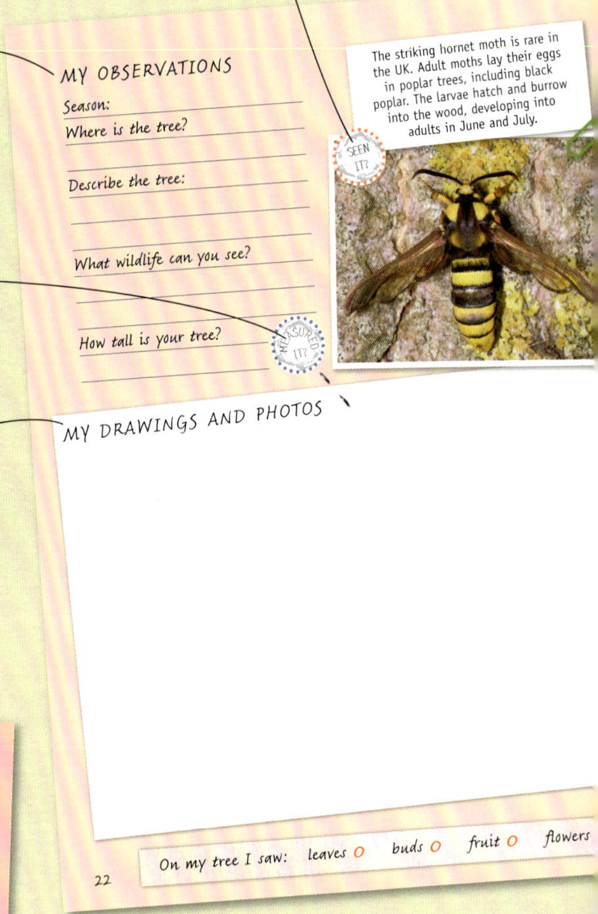


**Identifying a tree**

1 Look at the leaf... What basic leaf shape do you think it is – oval, long, hand-shaped, compound or needle?

2 Trees with similar leaf shapes are grouped together. The shape is shown in the top right of species.

3 Use the other illustrations to help you to confirm your identification.

**Scale guide**
Each tree in this book is compared against a person silhouette. This will help you to understand how big or small it actually is.

An average person is about 1.8 m in height

**Main text**
Every right-hand page introduces you to a species.

**Tree shape**
Refer to the tree shapes to help identify the tree at different times of the year.

**Leaf shape**
Flick through the book to find the correct leaf shape section. Each section is colour coded for easy navigation.

**Champion trees**
This tells you where you can see one of the biggest examples of the species in Britain.

**Fact file**
Provides vital statistics and information.

**Leaf and twig**
Use the leaf and twig to help identify the tree in summer or winter. (Evergreens do not have a winter twig because they don't lose their leaves.)

**Illustrations**
These show what the leaves, fruits and flowers of each species look like.

**Tick list**
Tick to record what you've seen on and around the tree.

## MY OBSERVATIONS

Season:

Where is the tree?

Describe the tree:

What wildlife can you see?

How tall is your tree?

MEASURED IT?

The brown roll-rim fungus can be found from late summer to autumn growing at the foot of deciduous trees, like alder. This fungus often grows near edible mushrooms, but is poisonous.

SEEN IT?

## MY DRAWINGS AND PHOTOS

On my tree I saw: leaves O buds O fruit O flowers O

# Alder *Alnus glutinosa*

The wood of the alder is fascinating – when it is submerged in water, it becomes as hard as stone. Much of the Italian city of Venice is built on piles of alder wood, which were sunk into the sand banks. Houses and other buildings were then built on top. The small, winged seeds of this water-loving tree get carried along by streams and rivers to grow further downstream. It is said that the green dye of the alder flower was used to colour the clothes of Robin Hood.

DECIDUOUS

**HEIGHT** 18–25 m

**WHERE** Widespread; woodland, hedgerows, often near water

**FLOWERING** February/March

**FRUITING** October–December

**LEAF TINT/FALL** November

**OTHER NAMES** Black alder, fearnog (Irish)

**USES** Canal lock gates, charcoal

CHAMPION TREE
CHATSWORTH PARK,
DERBYSHIRE
GIRTH 609 cm

insects o birds o mammals o fungi o other . . . . . . . .

## MY OBSERVATIONS

Season:

Where is the tree?

Describe the tree:

What wildlife can you see?

How tall is your tree?

MEASURED IT?

Great spotted woodpeckers are common in woodlands. Their colours and patterns make them easy to spot. Their tapping on tree trunks, including those of aspen, can be heard particularly in early spring.

SEEN IT?

## MY DRAWINGS AND PHOTOS

On my tree I saw: leaves O buds O fruit O flowers O

# Aspen *Populus tremula*



Fluttering leaves, which tremble in the breeze, give the aspen its Latin name *tremula* and its common name of 'quaking aspen'. The autumn-dry leaves of the aspen produce a rustling noise even in gentle breezes. Herbalists once used its flowers to treat people suffering from anxiety or nightmares. In Medieval times, the timber was used to make houses for the poor who could not afford oak. Charcoal made from aspen wood was used in the production of gunpowder.

DECIDUOUS

**HEIGHT** 15–25 m

**WHERE** Widespread; hillsides, hedgerows, often near water

**FLOWERING** March

**FRUITING** May

**LEAF TINT/FALL** October

**OTHER NAMES** Quaking aspen

**USES** Matches, paper, boxes for fruit and vegetables

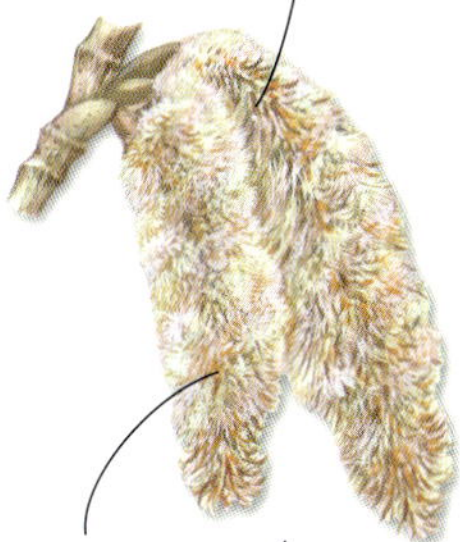

insects O birds O mammals O fungi O other . . . . . . . .

## MY OBSERVATIONS

Season:

Where is the tree?

Describe the tree:

What wildlife can you see?

How tall is your tree?

MEASURED IT?

Oyster fungi grow in forms called brackets on the trunks of beech and other deciduous trees. The topside is grey or cream, with white gills below. They are best seen in autumn.

SEEN IT?

## MY DRAWINGS AND PHOTOS

On my tree I saw: leaves O buds O fruit O flowers O

# Beech *Fagus sylvatica*



Beech trees have long been part of Britain's history, especially in the furniture-making industry. Particularly grand trees have been called 'queen beeches', and impressive beech woods are known as 'nature's cathedrals'. Since Roman times, beech wood was used for fuel and it was preferred for making furniture for its pink-orange colouring. Its nuts – called mast – were used as feed for animals.

DECIDUOUS

**CHAMPION TREE**
PLAS NEWYDD, ANGLESEY
GIRTH 962 cm

**HEIGHT** 10–35 m

**WHERE** Southern and eastern England, South Wales; woodland, chalky or sandy soils

**FLOWERING** April/May

**FRUITING** September–November

**LEAF TINT/FALL** November–April

**OTHER NAMES** Fea (Irish)

**USES** Furniture, kitchen utensils

insects ○ birds ○ mammals ○ fungi ○ other . . . . . . . . .

## MY OBSERVATIONS

Season:

Where is the tree?

Describe the tree:

What wildlife can you see?

How tall is your tree?

MEASURED IT?

The striking hornet moth is rare in the UK. Adult moths lay their eggs in poplar trees, including black poplar. The larvae hatch and burrow into the wood, developing into adults in June and July.

## MY DRAWINGS AND PHOTOS

On my tree I saw: leaves O buds O fruit O flowers O

# Black poplar *Populus nigra*

OVAL

Once common along riverbanks, today the native black poplar is very rare and found only in southern England and parts of Ireland. Black poplars are either male or female. Only a few hundred female trees exist in Britain and few of them grow near males. This means that seeds are rarely produced, so new trees are hard to find. Arrows found on the wreck of the Mary Rose were made of black poplar wood – they had survived 400 years beneath the sea.

DECIDUOUS

CHAMPION TREE
CHRIST'S COLLEGE, POWYS
GIRTH 685 cm

**HEIGHT** 20–25 m
**WHERE** Southern England, Ireland; often near water
**FLOWERING** March/April
**FRUITING** April/May
**LEAF TINT/FALL** October
**OTHER NAMES** Water poplar
**USES** Boat-building, floorboards

insects O birds O mammals O fungi O other . . . . . . . . .

## MY OBSERVATIONS

Season:

Where is the tree?

Describe the tree:

What wildlife can you see?

How tall is your tree?

MEASURED IT?

Dunnocks, also known as hedge sparrows, find shelter and berries to eat amongst blackthorn. Its branches grow tangled and spiny, making blackthorn a good tree for birds to build their nests.

SEEN IT?

## MY DRAWINGS AND PHOTOS

On my tree I saw: leaves ○ buds ○ fruit ○ flowers ○

# Blackthorn *Prunus spinosa*

This deciduous tree is distinctive because its flowers are some of the first to appear in spring, appearing even before its leaves. The fruits of the blackthorn are known as sloes and, although bitter to taste, they are popular with birds. It has long been considered a magical tree. In Celtic mythology it was home to fairies, and a blackthorn staff (long stick) was thought to be ideal for keeping evil spirits away.

**HEIGHT** 6–7 m

**WHERE** Widespread; woodland, scrubland, hedgerows

**FLOWERING** March/April

**FRUITING** August/September

**LEAF TINT/FALL** October/November

**OTHER NAMES** Sloe

**USES** Walking sticks, fruits used in food and drink

insects O birds O mammals O fungi O other . . . . . . . . .

## MY OBSERVATIONS

Season:

Where is the tree?

Describe the tree:

What wildlife can you see?

How tall is your tree?

MEASURED IT?

Box suckers are insects that spend winter as eggs on a box plant, hatching in spring. The larvae suck the tree's sap, making chemicals that stop the plant growing. Adults develop May to June.

## MY DRAWINGS AND PHOTOS

On my tree I saw: leaves O buds O fruit O flowers O

# Box *Buxus sempervirens*

Slow-growing and never gaining great height, box is considered to be more of a shrub than a tree. Its small, glossy, evergreen leaves grow tightly together, making it a perfect plant for garden hedges. Box can be cut and shaped into ornamental bushes in a practice known as topiary. It has an unpleasant smell, which caused Queen Anne (1665–1714) to have it removed from the gardens of Hampton Court Palace. Although common in gardens, box is rare in the wild.

EVERGREEN

**HEIGHT** 6–8 m

**WHERE** Southern England; gardens, chalky soils

**FLOWERING** January–May

**FRUITING** August/September

**LEAF TINT/FALL** Evergreen

**OTHER NAMES** Common box, boxwood

**USES** Kitchen tools, engraving

insects ○ birds ○ mammals ○ fungi ○ other . . . . . . . . .

## MY OBSERVATIONS

Season:

Where is the tree?

Describe the tree:

What wildlife can you see?

How tall is your tree?

MEASURED IT?

Brimstone butterflies lay their eggs on buckthorn leaves as this is the only plant eaten by the larvae. Adults hibernate over the winter and are one of the first butterflies to be seen in spring.

SEEN IT?

## MY DRAWINGS AND PHOTOS

On my tree I saw: leaves O buds O fruit O flowers O

# Buckthorn *Rhamnus cathartica*

OVAL

In the past, plants and trees were used to treat illnesses and buckthorn is no exception. The ripe, black berries are mildly poisonous to humans, but they are a good source of food for many birds. When herbal remedies were common, a tea made from buckthorn berries was used to treat a stomach ache, even though it causes vomiting and diarrhoea! Because of this, it is also referred to as purging buckthorn. The bark of a young tree is orange-brown and darkens with age.

DECIDUOUS

**HEIGHT** 4–6 m

**WHERE** Widespread; hedgerows, woodland

**FLOWERING** May/June

**FRUITING** September/October

**LEAF TINT/FALL** October/November

**OTHER NAMES** Common buckthorn, purging buckthorn

**USES** Carving, kitchen utensils

insects O birds O mammals O fungi O other . . . . . . . .

## MY OBSERVATIONS

Season:

Where is the tree?

Describe the tree:

What wildlife can you see?

How tall is your tree?

MEASURED IT?

The yellow-green lime aphid, *eucallipterus tiliae*, can be seen during the spring and summer months. Aphids are often regarded as pests because they feed on the tree's sap and can spread viruses.

SEEN IT?

## MY DRAWINGS AND PHOTOS

On my tree I saw: leaves O buds O fruit O flowers O

# Common lime *Tilia x europaea (vulgaris)*



The widely planted common lime is easy to spot as its leaves, and anything under them, get covered in a sticky substance called honeydew. Tiny insects called aphids suck sap (a sugary liquid) from the tree and produce honeydew. This attracts dirt, and by autumn, the leaves are sticky and filthy – and so are cars that may be parked beneath its branches. Beekeepers often place their hives near lime trees so that the bees produce 'lime honey'.

DECIDUOUS

**CHAMPION TREE**
HOLKER HALL, CUMBRIA
GIRTH 789 cm

**HEIGHT** 20–40 m

**WHERE** Widespread; woodland, parks, gardens, streets

**FLOWERING** July

**FRUITING** September

**LEAF TINT/FALL** October/ November

**OTHER NAMES** Common linden

**USES** Carving, model-building, guitar making

insects o birds o mammals o fungi o other . . . . . . . . .

## MY OBSERVATIONS

Season:

Where is the tree?

Describe the tree:

What wildlife can you see?

How tall is your tree?

MEASURED IT?

The autumn fruits of the crab apple tree attract greenfinches, along with many other birds. Greenfinches gather together in large flocks to feed, making lots of noise as they call to one another.

SEEN IT?

## MY DRAWINGS AND PHOTOS

On my tree I saw: leaves O buds O fruit O flowers O

# Crab apple *Malus sylvestis*

OVAL

Crab apples have been cultivated (grown especially) for hundreds of years, but a truly wild tree can be told apart by its thorns. These trees produce small, sour apples that are not good to eat raw. However, they are often made into tasty crab apple jellies and jams. Crab apple wood is hard, heavy and strong, making it ideal for items that endure heavy wear, such as tools and handles. The wood produces a pleasant scent when burnt.

DECIDUOUS

**HEIGHT** 7–9 m

**WHERE** Widespread, except Scotland; woodland, hedgerows

**FLOWERING** April/May

**FRUITING** September/October

**LEAF TINT/FALL** October/November

**OTHER NAMES** Wild crab

**USES** Carving, mallets, tool handles, fruits made into jelly

insects o birds o mammals o fungi o other . . . . . . . . .

## MY OBSERVATIONS

Season:

Where is the tree?

Describe the tree:

What wildlife can you see?

How tall is your tree?

MEASURED IT?

Robins often build their nests in hedgerows, including those of dogwood. Two broods of up to six blue eggs are laid from April to August. The berries also provide food for robins in autumn.

SEEN IT?

## MY DRAWINGS AND PHOTOS

On my tree I saw: leaves O buds O fruit O flowers O

# Dogwood *Cornus sanguinea*

OVAL

This small tree or shrub has red-tinted stems that are especially noticeable in winter when there are few colours to brighten the dark days. Dogwood has nothing to do with dogs. The wood is hard and was once used to make skewers known as 'dags'. This gave the tree its old name of dagswood. The leaves of dogwood can be identified by gently pulling them apart – a stringy latex can be seen where the veins have been broken.

**HEIGHT** 2–5 m

**WHERE** Widespread; woodland, scrubland, hedgerows

**FLOWERING** May/June

**FRUITING** September–November

**LEAF TINT/FALL** October/November

**OTHER NAMES** Bloodtwig

**USES** Skewers, arrow shafts, lamp oil can be made from fruits

insects o birds o mammals o fungi o other . . . . . . . . .

## MY OBSERVATIONS

Season:

Where is the tree?

Describe the tree:

What wildlife can you see?

How tall is your tree?

MEASURED IT?

Elm bark beetles can cause death to an elm. They spread Dutch elm disease – a fungus that infects the tree. The beetles chew holes into the wood to lay their eggs, and the larvae feed on wood.

SEEN IT?

## MY DRAWINGS AND PHOTOS

On my tree I saw: leaves O buds O fruit O flowers O

# English elm *Ulmus procera*



English elms were common in Britain, until the onset of Dutch elm disease killed 25 million of them in the 1970s. It is thought that this tree was introduced to Britain 2000 years ago by the Romans, and some scientific research suggests that all English elms descended from just one tree. This meant that many elms were equally vulnerable in the face of disease. Today, elms can often be seen growing in hedgerows.

**HEIGHT** 16–30 m

**WHERE** Widespread; woodland, hedgerows

**FLOWERING** February/March

**FRUITING** April–June

**LEAF TINT/FALL** October/November

**OTHER NAMES** Field elm

**USES** Before metal, the wood was used for water pipes

# MY OBSERVATIONS

Season:

Where is the tree?

Describe the tree:

What wildlife can you see?

How tall is your tree?

MEASURED IT?

The red underwing moth, which is often seen on willows, is only found in southern, central and eastern England. The moth's forewings look like bark, helping it to stay safe from predators.

# MY DRAWINGS AND PHOTOS

On my tree I saw: leaves O buds O fruit O flowers O

# Goat willow *Salix caprea*

OVAL

The goat willow is also known as 'pussy willow' because its springtime male catkins are soft and grey – like a cat's paw. Goat willows are important trees in woodland and hedgerows because they are closely associated with many types of butterfly and moth. Some larvae feed on the leaves and others live under the bark, feeding on the wood. As male catkins mature and turn yellow they are called 'goslings' because they are the same colour as baby geese.

DECIDUOUS

**HEIGHT** 4–10 m

**WHERE** Widespread; woodland, hedgerows

**FLOWERING** March/April

**FRUITING** May

**LEAF TINT/FALL** October/ November

**OTHER NAMES** Pussy willow, great swallow

**USES** Stems are used in basket-making

insects O birds O mammals O fungi O other . . . . . . . . .

## MY OBSERVATIONS

Season:

Where is the tree?

Describe the tree:

What wildlife can you see?

How tall is your tree?

MEASURED IT?

Like many birds, jays survive the winter by storing food. They collect and hide hazelnuts and acorns among leaf litter and moss on the ground. They dig them up months later to eat.

SEEN IT?

## MY DRAWINGS AND PHOTOS

On my tree I saw: leaves o buds o fruit o flowers o

# Hazel *Corylus avellana*

OVAL

As hazel catkins turn yellow it's a sign that spring is coming, and when squirrels start to gather hazelnuts winter is just around the corner. Hazels are not only a source of food for many types of wildlife, they provide homes and shelter for them too. They often grow in dense clusters with lots of stems growing from the ground, rather than a single trunk.

CHAMPION TREE
STOURHEAD, WILTSHIRE
GIRTH 248 cm

**HEIGHT** 12–15 m
**WHERE** Widespread; woodland, scrubland, hedgerows
**FLOWERING** February
**FRUITING** August/September
**LEAF TINT/FALL** November
**OTHER NAMES** Coll (Irish)
**USES** Walking sticks, stems used for fences and baskets

insects ○ birds ○ mammals ○ fungi ○ other . . . . . . . .

## MY OBSERVATIONS

Season:

Where is the tree?

Describe the tree:

What wildlife can you see?

How tall is your tree?

MEASURED IT?

Hawfinches can often be seen perching in the tops of trees, such as hornbeam. These birds have large, powerful bills that they use to crack open the hornbeam's tough nuts.

SEEN IT?

## MY DRAWINGS AND PHOTOS

On my tree I saw: leaves O buds O fruit O flowers O

# Hornbeam *Carpinus betulus*

OVAL

The statuesque hornbeam is an impressive deciduous tree with its pale, silvery-grey bark, and yellow-green catkins in the spring. It's often coppiced (stems cut back to the ground causing many long shoots to grow) or pollarded (top branches cut) and it is commonly planted for hedging. The white wood is very fine-grained, which makes particularly good firewood and charcoal. The Romans made their chariots from this wood because of its strength.

DECIDUOUS

CHAMPION TREE
HATFIELD FOREST, ESSEX
GIRTH 450 cm

**HEIGHT** 10–20 m

**WHERE** Southern and eastern England; woodland, hedgerows

**FLOWERING** March

**FRUITING** September

**LEAF TINT/FALL** November–April

**OTHER NAMES** Musclewood, ironwood

**USES** Chopping blocks, charcoal

long buds

male catkins are yellow-green with red specks

green female catkins develop into fruits

fruits are tough nuts with a three-lobed leaflet, or bract, attached

double-toothed edge with pointed tip

insects O birds O mammals O fungi O other . . . . . . . . .

## MY OBSERVATIONS

*Season:*

*Where is the tree?*

*Describe the tree:*

*What wildlife can you see?*

*How tall is your tree?*

MEASURED IT?

The seven-spotted ladybird is the most common ladybird in Europe. From February, they can be seen on plants, and trees such as mulberrys. Ladybirds hibernate in groups during winter.

## MY DRAWINGS AND PHOTOS

*On my tree I saw:* *leaves* O *buds* O *fruit* O *flowers* O

# Mulberry *Morus nigra*

OVAL

The black mulberry tree has a long history rooted in Southeast Asia, where it has been cultivated for thousands of years. It was introduced to Europe by the Romans, who dedicated the tree to Minerva, their goddess of wisdom. It has been widely planted and is grown in sheltered gardens for its delicious fruits, which contain a staining dye. It is celebrated in the nursery rhyme, 'Here we go round the mulberry bush'.

DECIDUOUS

**HEIGHT** 8–10 m

**WHERE** England; mostly gardens

**FLOWERING** May

**FRUITING** July

**LEAF TINT/FALL** October/ November

**OTHER NAMES** Black mulberry, Persian mulberry, sycamine tree

**USES** Fruits are eaten raw or made into jam

insects ○ birds ○ mammals ○ fungi ○ other . . . . . . . .

## MY OBSERVATIONS

Season:

Where is the tree?

Describe the tree:

What wildlife can you see?

How tall is your tree?

MEASURED IT?

Comma butterflies fly in late summer and early autumn and sometimes feed on fallen fruits, such as apples, pears and plums. The caterpillars feed on nettle, elm and hazel shoots.

SEEN IT?

## MY DRAWINGS AND PHOTOS

On my tree I saw: leaves O buds O fruit O flowers O

# Pear *Pyrus communis*

OVAL

The pear tree originally came from Southwest Asia, but it is now common throughout Europe. Pears have undergone many changes since they first arrived in Europe as farmers have cultivated sweeter and juicier varieties of the fruit. Pear trees can be found in gardens and orchards in Britain, especially southern areas. The wild pear, which is a different type of pear, is rare, and its fruits are hard, gritty and smaller than those of the *Pyrus communis*.

DECIDUOUS

**HEIGHT** 9–15 m

**WHERE** Southern England; orchards, woodland, gardens

**FLOWERING** March/April

**FRUITING** September/October

**LEAF TINT/FALL** November

**OTHER NAMES** Common pear, European pear

**USES** Wood is turned on a lathe to make bowls and similar objects

insects o birds o mammals o fungi o other . . . . . . . . .

## MY OBSERVATIONS

Season:

Where is the tree?

Describe the tree:

What wildlife can you see?

How tall is your tree?

MEASURED IT?

The larvae of the November moth feed on a wide range of trees, including plum and birch. Adult moths are hard to spot because their mottled grey-brown wings are perfectly camouflaged against bark.

SEEN IT?

## MY DRAWINGS AND PHOTOS

On my tree I saw: leaves O buds O fruit O flowers O

# Plum *Prunus domestica*

Plum trees are most commonly found growing in orchards and gardens. Plums were probably created as a hybrid (mix) of blackthorn and cherry plum. Today, plums are the second-most cultivated fruit in the world. The plum *Prunus domestica* is first mentioned in 479 BC in the writings of the Chinese philosopher Confucius – it is listed as a popular food in Chinese culture. A tree will not produce fruit until it is four or five years old. Dried fruits are known as prunes.

DECIDUOUS

**HEIGHT** 8–10 m

**LIFESPAN** 20–40 years

**WHERE** Mainly England; orchards, gardens

**FLOWERING** April/May

**FRUITING** July–September

**LEAF TINT/FALL** October/November

**OTHER NAMES** European plum

**USES** Grown for fruit

insects O birds O mammals O fungi O other . . . . . . . .

## MY OBSERVATIONS

Season:

Where is the tree?

Describe the tree:

What wildlife can you see?

How tall is your tree?

MEASURED IT?

The birch polypore fungus grows on the trunks of birch trees in a shape called a bracket. Unlike plants that use photosynthesis, fungi take nourishment from the tree using tiny organs called 'hyphae'.

## MY DRAWINGS AND PHOTOS

On my tree I saw: leaves O buds O fruit O flowers O

# Silver birch *Betula pendula*

OVAL

*With its silvery bark and fluttering leaves, the silver birch is sometimes called 'Queen of the forest'. It was one of the first trees to start growing back in Britain at the end of the Ice Age, around 10,000 years ago. It is known as a pioneer species, which means it is one of the first plants to grow in a new area. Silver birch produces huge crops of seeds of up to one million every year. This tree is easily recognisable by its bark, even in the winter.*

DECIDUOUS

CHAMPION TREE
PRIORY PARK, SURREY
GIRTH 399 cm

**HEIGHT** 18–25 m

**WHERE** Widespread; woodland, scrubland

**FLOWERING** April/May

**FRUITING** June

**LEAF TINT/FALL** November

**OTHER NAMES** Warty birch, beith (Irish)

**USES** Cotton reels

insects O birds O mammals O fungi O other . . . . . . . . .

## MY OBSERVATIONS

Season:

Where is the tree?

Describe the tree:

What wildlife can you see?

How tall is your tree?

MEASURED IT?

The green hairstreak butterfly can often be seen on plants, such as the wayfaring tree, searching for flowers. Like many butterflies, the adults feed on nectar – a sweet liquid produced by flowers.

SEEN IT?

## MY DRAWINGS AND PHOTOS

On my tree I saw: leaves O buds O fruit O flowers O

# Wayfaring tree *Viburnum lantana*

Once common alongside footpaths in southern England, the wayfaring tree grows in hedgerows, scrubland or on chalky ground. Today, it is a more common sight in gardens, grown for its ornamental leaves, large flower heads and bright berries. Despite their attractive appearance, the berries are mildly poisonous and should not be eaten. The young, flexible stems can be used to make twine.

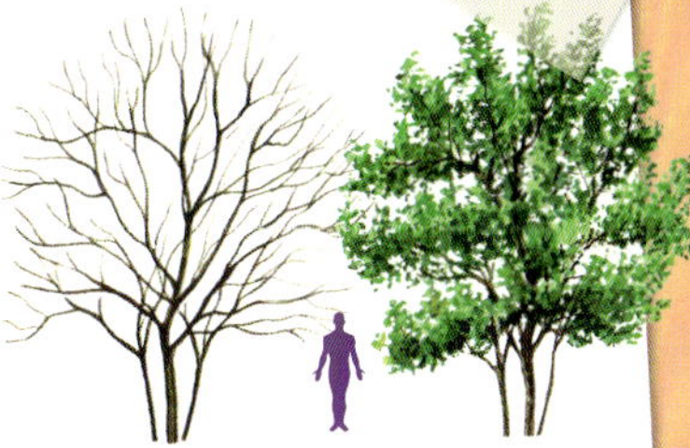

DECIDUOUS

**HEIGHT** Up to 6 m

**WHERE** South England, south Wales; hedgerows, scrubland, chalky soils

**FLOWERING** May

**FRUITING** August/September

**LEAF TINT/FALL** October/November

**OTHER NAMES** Hoarwithy

**USES** Young shoots can be made into twine

## MY OBSERVATIONS

Season:

Where is the tree?

Describe the tree:

What wildlife can you see?

How tall is your tree?

MEASURED IT?

Whitebeam berries attract many birds, including waxwings, which are winter visitors to Britain. These unusually tame birds have crests on their heads and waxy red spots on their wings.

## MY DRAWINGS AND PHOTOS

On my tree I saw: leaves ○ buds ○ fruit ○ flowers ○

# Whitebeam *Sorbus aria*

When the leaves of the whitebeam first open in the spring they appear white, giving this tree its name ('beam' is the Saxon word for tree). The whiteness is caused by the young leaves' soft coating of white hairs. Hair on the topside soon disappears as the leaves mature and droop downwards, but the undersides stay white. The wood of the whitebeam is very hard-wearing, and its small, red fruits can be made into jam and wine.

DECIDUOUS

**HEIGHT** 8–15 m

**WHERE** Southern England; woodland, chalky soils

**FLOWERING** May/June

**FRUITING** September

**LEAF TINT/FALL** October/ November

**OTHER NAMES** Common whitebeam

**USES** Tool handles, furniture

*insects* O *birds* O *mammals* O *fungi* O *other* . . . . . . . .

## MY OBSERVATIONS

Season:

Where is the tree?

Describe the tree:

What wildlife can you see?

How tall is your tree?

MEASURED IT?

Blackbirds are just one of many birds that flock around fruiting cherry trees to feed on their sweet fruits. Males are black with yellow beaks, and females are brown with spotted undersides.

SEEN IT?

## MY DRAWINGS AND PHOTOS

On my tree I saw: leaves O buds O fruit O flowers O

# Wild cherry *Prunus avium*

OVAL

When its branches are laden with white flowers or bunches of glossy fruits, the wild cherry attracts many birds. According to folklore, this tree has particular associations with cuckoos. The birds are believed to need three good meals of cherries before they will stop singing. The wood of a cherry tree is fine-grained and a beautiful shade of red, making it popular with cabinet makers.

DECIDUOUS

CHAMPION TREE
STUDLEY ROYAL & FOUNTAINS ABBEY, YORKSHIRE
GIRTH 572 cm

**HEIGHT** 18–25 m

**WHERE** Widespread; parks, woodland

**FLOWERING** April/May

**FRUITING** July/August

**LEAF TINT/FALL** October/November

**OTHER NAMES** Gean, crann silin (Irish)

**USES** Furniture, veneers (thin layer of wood used in furniture-making)

insects o birds o mammals o fungi o other . . . . . . . . .

## MY OBSERVATIONS

Season:

Where is the tree?

Describe the tree:

What wildlife can you see?

How tall is your tree?

MEASURED IT?

The privet hawk moth lays its eggs on the leaves of privet, ash and lilac. When the larvae hatch, they feed on the leaves. Its wings and body have pink, white and brown markings.

## MY DRAWINGS AND PHOTOS

On my tree I saw: leaves O buds O fruit O flowers O

# Wild privet *Ligustrum vulgare*

For centuries, gardeners have taken wild trees and shrubs, such as privet, and grown them as ornamental plants. Privet is one of few trees and shrubs that is described as being semi-evergreen. Depending on climate, sometimes it loses its leaves in winter and sometimes it doesn't. Privet is commonly grown in gardens and cut neatly into hedges, but the wild form looks very different, with long branches that reach upwards. The flowers and fruits were once used to treat eye and mouth diseases, despite being poisonous.

SEMI-EVERGREEN

**HEIGHT** 3–5 m

**WHERE** Southern and central England, Wales; gardens, streets, parks

**FLOWERING** May/June

**FRUITING** September/October

**LEAF TINT/FALL** Semi-evergreen

**USES** Planted for hedges

insects ○ birds ○ mammals ○ fungi ○ other . . . . . . . . .

## MY OBSERVATIONS

Season:

Where is the tree?

Describe the tree:

What wildlife can you see?

How tall is your tree?

MEASURED IT?

White-letter hairstreak butterflies only breed on elm. When these trees were struck down by disease in the 1970s, butterfly numbers dropped dramatically. The larvae of this butterfly are green.

SEEN IT?

## MY DRAWINGS AND PHOTOS

On my tree I saw: leaves ○ buds ○ fruit ○ flowers ○

# Wych elm *Ulmus glabra*

OVAL

In Middle English (a language spoken long ago) the word 'wych' meant bendy. Wych elm trees are not particularly bendy, but their young shoots are and they can be bent and twisted for making into baskets and other goods. These trees were badly affected by Dutch elm disease – a fungus carried by a wood-boring beetle. The leaves of the Wych elm are the largest of any native tree and can be up to 18 cm long!

DECIDUOUS

**HEIGHT** 16–30 m

**WHERE** Widespread; hedgerows, woodland

**FLOWERING** February/March

**FRUITING** May/June

**LEAF TINT/FALL** October/November

**OTHER NAMES** Scots elm

**USES** Chests, water troughs, sea defences

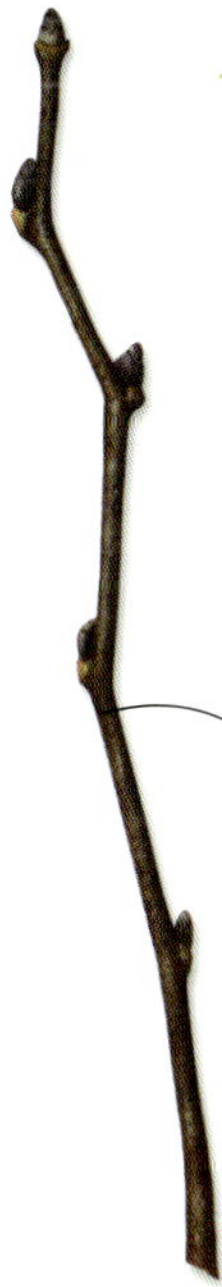

insects O birds O mammals O fungi O other . . . . . . . . .

## MY OBSERVATIONS

Season:

Where is the tree?

Describe the tree:

What wildlife can you see?

How tall is your tree?

MEASURED IT?

Holly blue butterflies lay two broods in the summer. The first brood is laid on holly and the second is laid on ivy. Both the caterpillars (larvae) and the adults feed on the leaves of both plants.

SEEN IT?

## MY DRAWINGS AND PHOTOS

On my tree I saw: leaves O buds O fruit O flowers O

# Holly *Ilix aquifolium*

With its clusters of bright red berries and prickly leaves, the holly tree is steeped in myth and mystery and is the subject of many superstitions. Although it was thought that cutting holly would bring bad luck, the custom of bringing holly into the home at midwinter goes back thousands of years. Hanging holly was thought to ward off evil spirits, and with its evergreen leaves, this tree was thought to symbolise fertility and be an effective charm against witches and goblins.

EVERGREEN

**HEIGHT** 8–15 m

**WHERE** Widespread; woodland, hedgerows, scrubland

**FLOWERING** April/May

**FRUITING** July

**LEAF TINT/FALL** Evergreen

**OTHER NAMES** Holm, cuileann (Irish)

**USES** Walking sticks, inlay work (in furniture-making), engraving

CHAMPION TREE
MEGGINCH CASTLE,
PERTH & KINROSS
GIRTH 300 cm

insects ○ birds ○ mammals ○ fungi ○ other . . . . . . . . .

## MY OBSERVATIONS

Season:

Where is the tree?

Describe the tree:

What wildlife can you see?

How tall is your tree?

MEASURED IT?

Wild rabbits are grey-brown in colour and are very common in the British countryside. In winter, when there is less food, they sometimes gnaw the bark of trees, including magnolia.

SEEN IT?

## MY DRAWINGS AND PHOTOS

On my tree I saw: leaves ○ buds ○ fruit ○ flowers ○

# Magnolia *Magnolia grandiflora*

**With their enormous, fragrant blooms and clusters of red seeds, magnolias are impressive trees that brighten up a garden.** They originally came from the United States and are the state flowers of Mississippi and Louisiana. Magnolias are normally fertilised by beetles. Its petals are unusually tough, which minimises damage by the crawling insects. They are named after Pierre Magnol (1638–1715), a French botanist, and many different varieties have been cultivated.

EVERGREEN

**HEIGHT** 12–25 m

**WHERE** Widespread; gardens, parks, arboretums

**FLOWERING** June–August

**FRUITING** September–December

**LEAF TINT/FALL** Evergreen

**OTHER NAMES** Southern evergreen magnolia

**USES** Veneers, vegetable crates

insects O  birds O  mammals O  fungi O  other . . . . . . . . .

## MY OBSERVATIONS

Season:

Where is the tree?

Describe the tree:

What wildlife can you see?

How tall is your tree?

MEASURED IT?

The gall wasp lays its eggs inside the oak tree. As a larva grows, a protective growth forms around it called a gall, or 'oak apple'. The larva stays inside the gall until it has developed into an adult.

SEEN IT?

## MY DRAWINGS AND PHOTOS

On my tree I saw: leaves O buds O fruit O flowers O

# Peduncluate oak *Quercus robur*

The pedunculate, or English, oak is known as the 'king of the forest' and it has a rich history, featuring in many myths and legends. English oaks provide a unique habitat for hundreds of species of other plants and animals. Oaks attract insects, which in turn attract birds, and acorns provide food for squirrels and other small mammals. A single tree can live for hundreds of years.

DECIDUOUS

**HEIGHT** 15–25 m

**WHERE** Widespread; ancient woodland

**FLOWERING** May

**FRUITING** October

**LEAF TINT/FALL** November

**OTHER NAMES** Common oak, dair (Irish), English oak

**USES** Building, furniture, floorboards

CHAMPION TREE
BOWTHORPE PARK FARM,
LINCOLNSHIRE
GIRTH 1279 cm

insects O birds O mammals O fungi O other . . . . . . . . .

## MY OBSERVATIONS

Season:

Where is the tree?

Describe the tree:

What wildlife can you see?

How tall is your tree?

MEASURED IT?

Fieldfares visit Britain in winter searching for food, and the berries from sea buckthorn are a good source. White flashes under their wings help identify these birds, which are a type of thrush.

SEEN IT?

## MY DRAWINGS AND PHOTOS

On my tree I saw: leaves O buds O fruit O flowers O

# Sea buckthorn *Hippophae rhamnoides*

This small, deciduous shrub can be found growing on exposed, windy coastlines in salty conditions that few other trees can tolerate. Sea buckthorn is an increasingly popular plant that is specially grown for the extraordinary properties of its bright orange berries and its deep and widespread roots. The berries are full of vitamin C and are used in skincare products. Its roots help to bind loose soil and add nitrogen to it, which is important for soil fertility.

DECIDUOUS

**HEIGHT** 1–3 m

**WHERE** Widespread; coastal areas, sand dunes

**FLOWERING** March/April

**FRUITING** September

**LEAF TINT/FALL** November

**USES** Skewers, fruits used in herbal medicines and cosmetics

insects ○ birds ○ mammals ○ fungi ○ other . . . . . . . .

## MY OBSERVATIONS

Season:

Where is the tree?

Describe the tree:

What wildlife can you see?

How tall is your tree?

MEASURED IT?

Small, green oak bush crickets are often seen in the leaves of oak trees, but they also live around other deciduous trees. They are most active after dark and are common from July to late autumn.

SEEN IT?

## MY DRAWINGS AND PHOTOS

On my tree I saw: leaves O buds O fruit O flowers O

# Sessile oak *Quercus petraea*

LONG

The sessile oak is one of just two native British oaks, but there are hundreds of different types in the northern hemisphere alone. The sessile oak is more likely to be found in stony uplands than the pedunculate oak, but they are similar in appearance. In Anglo-Saxon times, an oak was called an 'aik' and a seed was an 'aik-com', hence today's name – acorn. In one year, a mature oak tree may produce as many as 50,000 acorns.

DECIDUOUS

**HEIGHT** 15–30 m

**WHERE** Widespread; hillsides, woodland

**FLOWERING** April/May

**FRUITING** October/November

**LEAF TINT/FALL** November/December

**OTHER NAMES** Durmast oak, dair (Irish) darachor (Gaelic)

**USES** Building, poles, fences

CHAMPION TREE
COWDRAY PARK,
WEST SUSSEX
GIRTH 1253 cm

insects O birds O mammals O fungi O other . . . . . . . . .

## MY OBSERVATIONS

*Season:*

*Where is the tree?*

*Describe the tree:*

*What wildlife can you see?*

*How tall is your tree?*

MEASURED IT?

Also known as the hawthorn fly, the St Mark's fly lives around meadows and hedgerows on shrubs, including spindle. The female adults begin hatching around April 25th, which is St Mark's Day.

SEEN IT?

## MY DRAWINGS AND PHOTOS

*On my tree I saw:* *leaves* O *buds* O *fruit* O *flowers* O

# Spindle *Euonymus europaeus*

Spindles more often resemble bushes than trees, and they are often seen in hedgerows and woodlands. The timber of this plant was once used to make spindles – round, spinning pieces of wood that wool is wound onto. This gave the spindle tree its common name. The poisonous berries contain orange seeds that can be boiled to make a yellow dye. The berries have also been used in traditional remedies to cure farm animals of skin complaints.

DECIDUOUS

**HEIGHT** Up to 5 m

**WHERE** England, Wales; hedgerows, woodland

**FLOWERING** May/June

**FRUITING** September/October

**LEAF TINT/FALL** October/November

**OTHER NAMES** Fusanum, fusoria, prickwood, skewerwood

**USES** Skewers, spindles, knitting needles

insects O birds O mammals O fungi O other . . . . . . . . .

## MY OBSERVATIONS

Season:

Where is the tree?

Describe the tree:

What wildlife can you see?

How tall is your tree?

MEASURED IT?

Grey squirrels have been commonly found in the UK, ever since they were introduced in the early 1900s. Their fur is grey, sometimes with brown tinges. Nutritious sweet chestnuts are one source of food for grey squirrels.

## MY DRAWINGS AND PHOTOS

On my tree I saw: leaves O buds O fruit O flowers O

# Sweet chestnut *Castanea sativa*

LONG

These trees produce large, edible nuts that can be roasted and are often sold in streets, at fairs and other winter events. Sweet chestnuts have been long associated with winter festivals and were once seen as sources of magic. They are native to the warmer parts of Europe and were first brought to Britain by Roman soldiers, who relied on the nuts as an important part of their diet. Sweet chestnuts do not always ripen fully in Britain.

DECIDUOUS

**HEIGHT** 20–30 m

**WHERE** Widespread; woodland, parks, well-drained soil

**FLOWERING** June/July

**FRUITING** October/November

**LEAF TINT/FALL** October–December

**OTHER NAMES** Spanish chestnut

**USES** Stems used for fence poles, nuts roasted for eating

CHAMPION TREE
CANFORD SCHOOL, DORSET
GIRTH 1344 cm

insects O birds O mammals O fungi O other . . . . . . . . .

## MY OBSERVATIONS

*Season:*

*Where is the tree?*

*Describe the tree:*

*What wildlife can you see?*

*How tall is your tree?*

MEASURED IT?

The beautiful song of a willow warbler marks the beginning of spring. These pretty birds visit Britain from April to October, and often perch in willow and birch trees looking for insects.

## MY DRAWINGS AND PHOTOS

*On my tree I saw:* *leaves* O *buds* O *fruit* O *flowers* O

# White willow *Salix alba*

The white willow grows well in damp soil and so is most likely to be found alongside streams and ponds, often near alder trees. Animals, especially horses, enjoy nibbling the leaves and tender shoots of this tree. The pale brown wood of the white willow burns easily and quickly. This tree can be pollarded every four or five years to produce a crop of straight poles, which are used for making fences.

DECIDUOUS

**HEIGHT** 20–25 m

**WHERE** Widespread; often near water

**FLOWERING** April/May

**FRUITING** June–August

**LEAF TINT/FALL** October/November

**OTHER NAMES** European willow, sailach (Irish)

**USES** Medicine made from bark and leaves is similar to asprin

insects O birds O mammals O fungi O other . . . . . . . . .

## MY OBSERVATIONS

Season:

Where is the tree?

Describe the tree:

What wildlife can you see?

How tall is your tree?

MEASURED IT?

Sycamore moths have a wingspan of up to 4.5 cm. They are pale to dark grey in colour, and have a mottled pattern that helps to camouflage them. These moths feed on sycamores, maples and horse chestnuts.

SEEN IT?

## MY DRAWINGS AND PHOTOS

On my tree I saw: leaves O buds O fruit O flowers O

# Field Maple *Acer campestre*

The field maple provides an ideal habitat for many small creatures, and plants such as lichens and mosses. Field maples are often found growing in hedgerows. In autumn, they can be identified by their leaves, which turn red and yellow. According to ancient myths, a child could be guaranteed a long life by being passed through the branches of a field maple. In some places, it was thought that field maples could protect a house against bats.

DECIDUOUS

**HEIGHT** 8–14 m

**WHERE** Widespread; woodland, hedgerows

**FLOWERING** April

**FRUITING** June/July

**LEAF TINT/FALL** November

**OTHER NAMES** Hedge maple, English maple

**USES** Wood used in violin-making

CHAMPION TREE
DOWNHAM CHURCHYARD, ESSEX
GIRTH 452 cm

insects O birds O mammals O fungi O other . . . . . . . . .

## MY OBSERVATIONS

Season:

Where is the tree?

Describe the tree:

What wildlife can you see?

How tall is your tree?

MEASURED IT?

Bullfinches are shy birds that hide in thickets and hedges, such as guelder rose, but their low, clear whistle may give them away. They eat buds, berries and seeds.

SEEN IT?

## MY DRAWINGS AND PHOTOS

On my tree I saw: leaves O buds O fruit O flowers O

# Guelder rose *Viburnum opulus*

Despite its name, this shrub is not a rose at all, but more closely related to the elder. Its unusual name comes from the Dutch province of Guelderland where it was grown as a decorative garden plant. Guelder rose berries are popular with birds, such as bullfinches, and small animals, but they are poisonous to humans. The berries can be used to make a red ink.

DECIDUOUS

**HEIGHT** Up to 4 m

**WHERE** Widespread; woodland, scrubland, hedgerows, damp soils

**FLOWERING** June/July

**FRUITING** September

**LEAF TINT/FALL** October/November

**OTHER NAMES** Snowball bush

**USES** Skewers

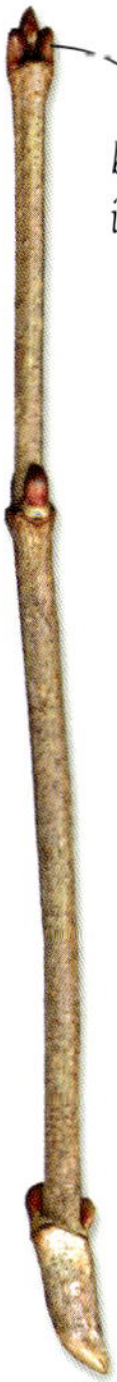

insects ○ birds ○ mammals ○ fungi ○ other . . . . . . . . .

## MY OBSERVATIONS

Season:

Where is the tree?

Describe the tree:

What wildlife can you see?

How tall is your tree?

MEASURED IT?

The hawthorn shield bug has brown markings on its broad, shield-shaped back. It's common on hawthorn leaves, but also feeds on other types of shrub and tree, including oaks and whitebeam.

## MY DRAWINGS AND PHOTOS

On my tree I saw: leaves ○ buds ○ fruit ○ flowers ○

# Hawthorn *Crataegus monogyna*

HAND-SHAPED

*The hawthorn's frothy white blossom is a sign that summer is on its way. Hawthorn is a popular hedgerow plant and its leaves are quick to appear in spring. In folklore, in North Wales, hawthorn was associated with death, possibly because the flowers' scent reminds some people of rotting flesh. However the berries, leaves and flowers have been used in many past medicines. It also has long associations with May Day – its wood was used to make the first Maypoles.*

DECIDUOUS

CHAMPION TREE
HETHEL, NORFOLK
GIRTH 245 cm

**HEIGHT** 12–15 m

**WHERE** Widespread; hedgerows, shrubland

**FLOWERING** May/June

**FRUITING** March/April

**LEAF TINT/FALL** November

**OTHER NAMES** May, whitethorn, quickthorn, tramp's supper, holy innocents

**USES** Walking sticks, tool handles

insects O birds O mammals O fungi O other . . . . . . . . .

## MY OBSERVATIONS

Season:

Where is the tree?

Describe the tree:

What wildlife can you see?

How tall is your tree?

MEASURED IT?

Honey bees visit flowers, such as those of horse chestnut, for nectar. They also carry pollen on their bodies to other flowers. This helps fertilise the flowers so that they will produce seeds.

SEEN IT?

## MY DRAWINGS AND PHOTOS

On my tree I saw: leaves O buds O fruit O flowers O

# Horse chestnut *Aesculus hippocastanum*



Horse chestnuts are best known for their glossy, brown nuts known as conkers. Competitors meet up in Northamptonshire every year to battle in the World Conker Championships – an event that has been running since 1965. Horse chestnut trees arrived in Britain in the 16th century and possibly get their name from the practice of feeding conkers to horses to cure them of illness.

DECIDUOUS

**HEIGHT** 14–28 m

**WHERE** Widespread; woodland, parks, hedgerows

**FLOWERING** May

**FRUITING** September/October

**LEAF TINT/FALL** October/ November

**OTHER NAMES** Conker tree

**USES** Extract from nuts is used to make herbal medicines

sticky buds

flowers have five petals and a small pink spot near the centre

upright spikes of white flowers

five to seven long leaflets appear in early spring

leaflets fan out and are on a sturdy stalk

about 6 cm wide

one brown nut, (conker), inside each spiky green fruit

*insects* O *birds* O *mammals* O *fungi* O *other* . . . . . . . . .

## MY OBSERVATIONS

Season:

Where is the tree?

Describe the tree:

What wildlife can you see?

How tall is your tree?

MEASURED IT?

House sparrows used to be more common in towns and cities, perching in trees such as London planes. In recent years, their numbers have dropped. They feed on insects, seeds, berries and buds.

SEEN IT?

## MY DRAWINGS AND PHOTOS

On my tree I saw: leaves O buds O fruit O flowers O

# London plane *Platanus x hispanica*

HAND-SHAPED

London plane trees are a familiar sight in many cities and towns. They were widely planted along streets in urban areas because they tolerate pollution. In the 17th century, American plane and oriental plane trees were cross-bred to produce this new variety. The London plane sheds dirt in it's bark, which peels off through the year revealing a paler yellow bark beneath. Its attractive, hard-wearing timber is also known as 'lacewood'.

DECIDUOUS

**HEIGHT** 13–35 m

**WHERE** Widespread; streets, parks, cities, towns

**FLOWERING** May/June

**FRUITING** September/October

**LEAF TINT/FALL** October/November

**OTHER NAMES** Hybrid plane

**USES** Furniture

insects o birds o mammals o fungi o other . . . . . . . . .

## MY OBSERVATIONS

Season:

Where is the tree?

Describe the tree:

What wildlife can you see?

How tall is your tree?

MEASURED IT?

In winter, the large, oval outline of a tawny owl may be seen against the branches of a sycamore tree. Owls have brilliant eyesight and hearing.

SEEN IT?

## MY DRAWINGS AND PHOTOS

On my tree I saw: leaves O buds O fruit O flowers O

# Sycamore *Acer pseudoplatanus*

In the autumn, sycamores produce thousands of spinning, winged fruits called 'keys'. The wings act like helicopter blades and spin the keys through the air so that they land a distance from the tree. The sycamore is also known as the martyrs' tree. In England in 1834, a group of workers – the Tolpuddle Martyrs – met under a sycamore to form a society to fight for better wages. They were expelled from the country as punishment.

DECIDUOUS

**HEIGHT** 16–35 m

**WHERE** Widespread; woodland, hedgerows, mountains

**FLOWERING** April/May

**FRUITING** September

**LEAF TINT/FALL** October/November

**OTHER NAMES** Great maple, great plane, martyrs' tree

**USES** Furniture, veneers, musical instruments

each individual flower has five petals

yellow-green flowers hang in spikes

winged fruits, or keys, are green at first, then ripen to brown

each key holds two seeds

green buds grow in opposite pairs

up to 15 cm long with five lobes

stalks are often red

CHAMPION TREE
BIRNAM, PERTH & KINROSS
GIRTH 723 cm

insects O birds O mammals O fungi O other . . . . . . . . .

## MY OBSERVATIONS

Season:

Where is the tree?

Describe the tree:

What wildlife can you see?

How tall is your tree?

MEASURED IT?

Redwings may be seen flying in flocks in autumn. These birds are a type of thrush and they eat insects, as well as berries from trees, such as rowan, hawthorn and the wild service tree.

## MY DRAWINGS AND PHOTOS

On my tree I saw: leaves O buds O fruit O flowers O

# Wild service tree *Sorbus torminalis*

The wild service tree is an indicator of ancient woodland – areas where there has been continuous woodland since at least 1600. In spring, white blossom covers this tree and in autumn, its leaves turn copper-red. Its berries, which were used to cure stomach upsets until the 1700s, are best eaten when overripe. This tree also goes by the name of 'chequers'. Some say this refers to the bark peeling off in squares and leaving a chequerboard effect.

DECIDUOUS

**HEIGHT** 10–25 m

**WHERE** Southern England, Wales; ancient woodland

**FLOWERING** May/June

**FRUITING** September–November

**LEAF TINT/FALL** October/November

**OTHER NAMES** Chequers

**USES** Fruits used to make an alcoholic drink called 'Chequers'

insects O birds O mammals O fungi O other . . . . . . . . .

## MY OBSERVATIONS

Season:

Where is the tree?

Describe the tree:

What wildlife can you see?

How tall is your tree?

MEASURED IT?

King Alfred's cake fungus is also called coal fungus. It is ball-shaped and dark in colour. It grows on fallen trees, especially ash and beech. Dried fungus makes good tinder for fires.

## MY DRAWINGS AND PHOTOS

On my tree I saw: leaves O buds O fruit O flowers O

# Ash *Fraxinus excelsior*

The stately ash is one of the tallest deciduous trees in Europe and it grows easily in many habitats across Britain. In Scandinavian mythology, the ash was regarded as the tree of life. In English folklore, it was used to predict the weather. If oak buds opened before ash buds then the summer would be dry, but if ash buds opened first, the summer would be wet. Like many trees, the ash was once believed to provide defence against black magic and witchcraft.

**HEIGHT** 15–30 m

**WHERE** Widespread; woodland, hedgerows, hillsides

**FLOWERING** April

**FRUITING** June

**LEAF TINT/FALL** September/October

**OTHER NAMES** Lofty ash, fuinnseog (Irish)

**USES** Oars, farm tools, spade handles

CHAMPION TREE
MOCCAS PARK, HEREFORDSHIRE
GIRTH 825 cm

insects O birds O mammals O fungi O other . . . . . . . . .

## MY OBSERVATIONS

Season:

Where is the tree?

Describe the tree:

What wildlife can you see?

How tall is your tree?

MEASURED IT?

Jelly ear fungus is a rubbery, ear-shaped fungus that is dark in colour. It often grows on dead elder and elm trees and is best seen in winter and spring. Each lobe can grow up to 10 cm across.

SEEN IT?

## MY DRAWINGS AND PHOTOS

On my tree I saw: leaves O buds O fruit O flowers O

# Elder *Sambucus nigra*

COMPOUND

The elder has proved to be a useful British tree, with the flowers, berries and stems all being put to good use. 'Elder' comes from the Anglo Saxon word 'aeld', meaning 'fire'. The stems are hollow and were once used to blow air into fires. In Denmark, the tree was associated with magic and, before a tree could be cut down, permission had to be sought from its spirit. The flowers can be made into a cordial and the berries into wine.

DECIDUOUS

**HEIGHT** Up to 10 m

**WHERE** Widespread; hedgerows, scrubland

**FLOWERING** June/July

**FRUITING** August/September

**LEAF TINT/FALL** October/November

**OTHER NAMES** Elderflower, common elder, black elder

**USES** Toys, wooden spoons

insects o birds o mammals o fungi o other . . . . . . . . .

## MY OBSERVATIONS

Season:

Where is the tree?

Describe the tree:

What wildlife can you see?

How tall is your tree?

MEASURED IT?

The buff-tip moth avoids predators by resting on a stem to look like a broken twig. The yellow-black larvae of this moth feeds on the leaves of deciduous trees, including laburnum.

SEEN IT?

## MY DRAWINGS AND PHOTOS

On my tree I saw: leaves ○ buds ○ fruit ○ flowers ○

# Laburnum *Laburnum anagyroides*

COMPOUND

A common sight in British gardens, laburnum is recognisable by its cascades of bright yellow flowers in the summer. It originated in Europe and was introduced to Britain in the 16th century. All parts of the tree are poisonous, especially the seeds. The heartwood is deep brown in colour and was highly prized for making decorative items. It was often used as a substitute for the dark wood of the tropical ebony tree.

**HEIGHT** 6–9 m

**WHERE** Widespread; parks, gardens

**FLOWERING** May/June

**FRUITING** September/October

**LEAF TINT/FALL** October–December

**OTHER NAMES** Goldenchain, goldenrain

**USES** Grown for ornament

insects O birds O mammals O fungi O other . . . . . . . . .

## MY OBSERVATIONS

Season:

Where is the tree?

Describe the tree:

What wildlife can you see?

How tall is your tree?

MEASURED IT?

The rowan tree's ripening red berries provide a feast for many birds, such as the mistle thrush. They visit berry-laden trees in winter, and will often defend a tree from other birds.

SEEN IT?

## MY DRAWINGS AND PHOTOS

On my tree I saw: leaves O buds O fruit O flowers O

# Rowan *Sorbus aucuparia*

The magical rowan tree has a past steeped in history and mythology. 'Rowan' comes from the old Norse word for tree – 'raun'. Its wood was used by druids to make staffs and wands. People used to put sprigs of rowan in their houses to protect them from lightning, and sailors took it on board boats to protect them from storms. Raw berries are poisonous, but once cooked they can be eaten. As well as food and drink, they have been used in herbal medicines.

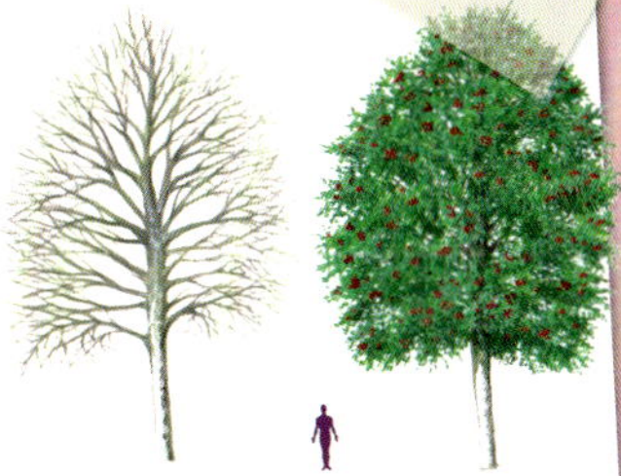

DECIDUOUS

**HEIGHT** 8–15 m
**WHERE** Widespread; mountains, parks, gardens
**FLOWERING** May
**FRUITING** October/November
**LEAF TINT/FALL** October/November
**OTHER NAMES** Mountain ash, whispering tree, witchbane
**USES** Bows, tool handles, bowls

*purple-brown buds are covered in grey hairs*

*orange-red berries up to 1 cm long*

*each fruit contains one or two seeds*

*small, cream-coloured flowers grow in dense clusters*

*five to eight pairs of leaflets*

*orange and reddish-brown in autumn*

CHAMPION TREE
COTHERSTONE, DURHAM
GIRTH 340 cm

*insects* ○ *birds* ○ *mammals* ○ *fungi* ○ *other* . . . . . . . .

## MY OBSERVATIONS

Season:

Where is the tree?

Describe the tree:

What wildlife can you see?

How tall is your tree?

MEASURED IT?

Codling moths lay their eggs in June on the leaves or fruits of fruit trees, such as apple, pear and walnut. The larvae burrow into the fruit to eat. Once full, they eat their way out.

SEEN IT?

## MY DRAWINGS AND PHOTOS

On my tree I saw: leaves O buds O fruit O flowers O

# Walnut *Juglans regia*

Walnut trees have been grown in Britain for their nuts, but also for their timber, which is one of the most beautiful woods in the world. There is evidence that walnuts have been growing in Britain since at least Roman times, and they were widely planted in the 1800s. Thousands of walnut trees were felled in the Napoleonic wars so that the timber could be used to make guns for soldiers.

DECIDUOUS

**HEIGHT** 10–30 m

**WHERE** Southern England; woodland, parks

**FLOWERING** April–June

**FRUITING** September/October

**LEAF TINT/FALL** October/ November

**OTHER NAMES** Persian walnut, common walnut

**USES** Furniture, veneers, nuts eaten as food

insects ○ birds ○ mammals ○ fungi ○ other . . . . . . . . .

# MY OBSERVATIONS

Season:

Where is the tree?

Describe the tree:

What wildlife can you see?

How tall is your tree?

MEASURED IT?

Starlings are noisy, colourful birds that flock around tall trees, such as cedars. They nest in tree cavities, and often hop around the ground near tree roots searching for ants and other bugs.

# MY DRAWINGS AND PHOTOS

On my tree I saw: leaves O buds O fruit O flowers O

# Cedar of Lebanon *Cedrus libani*

NEEDLE

This cedar is native to the mountain forests of the eastern Mediterranean, and has been a popular tree to plant in parkland and large gardens in the UK. In ancient times, many of the cedar forests in Lebanon were felled to supply timber for building materials and fuel. Some stories tell of how it was first brought to Europe in the 18th century by a Frenchman, who uprooted a seedling while travelling in the Middle East. Not having a flowerpot he stored the young tree in his hat, looking after it until his return to Paris.

EVERGREEN

**HEIGHT** 8–35 m

**WHERE** Widespread; parks, large gardens, churchyards

**FLOWERING** June–September

**FRUITING** August–October

**LEAF TINT/FALL** Evergreen

**OTHER NAMES** Lebanese cedar

**USES** Buildings, furniture

insects O birds O mammals O fungi O other . . . . . . . . .

# MY OBSERVATIONS

Season:

Where is the tree?

Describe the tree:

What wildlife can you see?

How tall is your tree?

MEASURED IT?

The common crossbill belongs to the finch family, and is often found near conifers, such as larches, as they eat the seeds. Crossbills make their nests out of twigs, moss, wool and hair.

SEEN IT?

# MY DRAWINGS AND PHOTOS

On my tree I saw: leaves ○ buds ○ fruit ○ flowers ○

# European larch *Larix decidua*

Larches grow tall and straight and, unusually for conifers, they lose their leaves in the autumn. These fast-growing trees produce good quality timber and they are often seen growing in plantations. In Siberia, it was once believed that man was created from a larch tree, and that woman was created separately from a conifer or fir tree. Herbalists use a weak tea made from the inner bark to treat stomach upsets and asthma.

DECIDUOUS

**HEIGHT** 12–30 m

**WHERE** Widespread; woodland, parks, gardens, plantations

**FLOWERING** March/April

**FRUITING** September

**LEAF TINT/FALL** October/November

**OTHER NAMES** Common larch

**USES** Fences, furniture, boat-building

*insects* ○ *birds* ○ *mammals* ○ *fungi* ○ *other* . . . . . . . . .

## MY OBSERVATIONS

Season:

Where is the tree?

Describe the tree:

What wildlife can you see?

How tall is your tree?

MEASURED IT?

Treecreepers have long toes that allow them to hang upside down and scuttle quickly up a tree. They have brown-and-white mottled feathers, and are known to roost in sequoia trunks.

SEEN IT?

## MY DRAWINGS AND PHOTOS

On my tree I saw: leaves O buds O fruit O flowers O

# Giant sequoia *Sequioadendron giganteum*

The giant sequoia is one of the tallest-growing plants in the world and is also one of the longest living, capable of surviving up to 4000 years. The tallest specimen is the General Sherman in the United States, which, in 1987, measured 83.8 m tall. Giant sequoias come from California and were brought to Britain in 1853, the year that the Duke of Wellington died. This is how this tree got its other name – Wellingtonia. The yew is one of few trees known to survive to a similar age.

EVERGREEN

**HEIGHT** 20–50 m

**WHERE** Widespread; parks, grounds of historic buildings

**FLOWERING** May/June

**FRUITING** All year

**LEAF TINT/FALL** Evergreen

**OTHER NAMES** Mammoth tree, Wellingtonia

**USES** Leaves used in wreaths, and floral displays

insects O birds O mammals O fungi O other . . . . . . . . .

## MY OBSERVATIONS

Season:

Where is the tree?

Describe the tree:

What wildlife can you see?

How tall is your tree?

MEASURED IT?

The juniper carpet moth feeds mainly on juniper trees. These insects are only found in a few places in Britain and they are very well camouflaged. They fly from October to November.

SEEN IT?

## MY DRAWINGS AND PHOTOS

On my tree I saw: leaves O buds O fruit O flowers O

# Juniper *Juniperus communis*

Juniper is a small, slow-growing, evergreen tree and can be found in a wide range of habitats all around the world. Its fruits can take two to three years to ripen, so you may see black and green berries on the same tree. These are actually soft cones rather than true berries. As birds eat them and fly to other trees, they help distribute the seeds. In folklore, in parts of southwest England, the wood and needles were burned near a sick person – this was thought to cure infection.

EVERGREEN

**HEIGHT** 5–10 m

**WHERE** Mainly southern England; woodland, scrubland, chalky soils

**FLOWERING** May/June

**FRUITING** All year

**LEAF TINT/FALL** Evergreen

**OTHER NAMES** Common juniper, dwarf juniper

**USES** Wood used to smoke meat, fruits used to flavour gin

*insects* ○ *birds* ○ *mammals* ○ *fungi* ○ *other . . . . . . . . .*

## MY OBSERVATIONS

Season:

Where is the tree?

Describe the tree:

What wildlife can you see?

How tall is your tree?

MEASURED IT?

Coal tits are often seen near Norway spruces and other conifer trees. These tiny birds form large flocks in autumn and winter, in search of food, such as insects and seeds.

SEEN IT?

## MY DRAWINGS AND PHOTOS

On my tree I saw: leaves O buds O fruit O flowers O

# Norway spruce *Picea abies*

It is believed that the Norway spruce was growing in Britain long before the last Ice Age. This species did not return to Britain until around the 1500s when it was brought over from Europe. It is grown in plantations for timber and also for use as Christmas trees. The German tradition of decorating Christmas trees became fashionable in England in the 19th century after Queen Victoria married the German nobleman, Prince Albert.

EVERGREEN

**HEIGHT** 18–40 m

**WHERE** Widespread; plantations parks

**FLOWERING** May

**FRUITING** September–November

**LEAF TINT/FALL** Evergreen

**OTHER NAMES** Spruce fir

**USES** Timber, paper, Christmas trees

insects O birds O mammals O fungi O other . . . . . . . . .

## MY OBSERVATIONS

Season:

Where is the tree?

Describe the tree:

What wildlife can you see?

How tall is your tree?

MEASURED IT?

Wood ants live in colonies of up to half a million individuals. Some make their nests by piling up pine needles and other plant matter. They are reddish-brown in colour and up to 1 cm long.

SEEN IT?

## MY DRAWINGS AND PHOTOS

On my tree I saw: leaves O buds O fruit O flowers O

# Scots pine *Pinus sylvestris*

There are many conifers growing in Britain today, but the Scots pine is native to parts of Scotland, making it the only native British pine. These fast-growing trees are found from Spain to Siberia. Scots pine trees grow tall and straight, and the wood is very hard-wearing, which makes it ideal for use as telegraph poles. Long ago, the wood was used in ship-making and for water pipes. The cones have been used to forecast weather – it is thought that when the cones open the air is dry, so no rain should be expected.

CHAMPION TREE
MUIRWARD WOOD,
PERTH & KINROSS
GIRTH 628 cm

**HEIGHT** 12–36 m

**WHERE** Widespread; woodland, plantations

**FLOWERING** April

**FRUITING** April

**LEAF TINT/FALL** Evergreen

**OTHER NAMES** Scots fir, giuis (Irish)

**USES** Fences, flooring, telegraph poles, railway sleepers

insects O birds O mammals O fungi O other . . . . . . . . .

## MY OBSERVATIONS

Season:

Where is the tree?

Describe the tree:

What wildlife can you see?

How tall is your tree?

MEASURED IT?

Nuthatches are small birds with strong feet and ultra-sharp claws, and they are able to run head first down a tree trunk. They are one of many birds that may be seen in yew trees eating the fruits.

SEEN IT?

## MY DRAWINGS AND PHOTOS

On my tree I saw: leaves O buds O fruit O flowers O

# Yew *Taxus baccata*

The dark, mysterious yew tree has been the subject of myths and legends for centuries, and it can often be found in cemeteries and church grounds. Known to live for hundreds – sometimes thousands – of years, several churchyard yews are more than 1000 years old. In ancient times, people planted yews where they would be buried. Most parts of a yew tree are extremely poisonous to humans and animals.

EVERGREEN

**HEIGHT** 4–20 m

**WHERE** Widespread; churchyards, woodland

**FLOWERING** March/April

**FRUITING** October

**LEAF TINT/FALL** Evergreen

**OTHER NAMES** Iur (Irish)

**USES** Furniture, tool handles, an anti-cancer drug is made from the leaves

CHAMPION TREE
ULCOMBE PARISH CHURCH, KENT
GIRTH 990 cm

insects o birds o mammals o fungi o other . . . . . . . . .

# WILDFLOWERS

# Introducing Wildflowers

*Wildflowers are so much more than pretty things that beautify our hedgerows, fields, woods and nature reserves.*

*They are the foundations on which all ecosystems are built, from the soil in which they grow to the food and shelter they provide for the wild animals that live among their foliage and feed on their leaves, buds, stems and roots. Put names to the wildflowers growing in a certain area and you will start to gain a deeper understanding of every ecosystem you walk through or visit.*

*This section should help you put a name to a flower. Many widespread species are included, as well as a few that are so spectacular they simply had to make the pages.*

*There are over 40 wildflower species to discover here. Organised by colour, each species is clearly presented, and there's also space for your photos, sketches and notes. There's instructions on how to become a wildflower detective, including a checklist of the equipment you will need.*

*Hopefully by using this guide you'll start to see wildflowers as part of a bigger picture – the first step towards understanding whole habitats.*

Nick Baker

# What is a flower?

A flower develops inside a bud. Within the petals is a ring of male parts (stamens). Each has a filament topped by an anther containing the male reproductive cells inside pollen grains. At the centre of the flower are the female parts – the stigma and the style. The style widens at its base into an ovary, containing the female reproductive cells in their ovules (eggs).

**Pollination:** This takes place when an anther releases its pollen, some grains of which travel to the stigma. This allows the male cells in the pollen to reach the female cells in the ovules and fertilise them. Pollen can be carried by wind, animals or by water.

**Fruit and seeds:** After fertilisation, the ovule turns into a seed and the ovary turns into a fruit, such as this cherry. The fruit may become brightly coloured so it is eaten, or dry up and form parachutes or wings to enable it to be blown away.

# About Wildlife Watch

## www.wildlifewatch.org.uk

If you want to find out more about the UK's wildlife then take a look at The Wildlife Trusts' website for children and families.

Log in to create a profile and start collecting nature stars for spotting wildlife, keeping an online nature diary, or uploading photos.

Make nature spotting sheets, play games and enjoy fun downloads. The activity database has loads of ideas, from colouring sheets to instructions for how to make a butterfly feeder.

The online database features more than 850 species

Wood anemones often grow in ancient woodlands. If you spot some, record your sighting online

There's also a page for each Wildlife Trust in the UK, where you can find out about nature reserves near you and discover local Wildlife Watch groups. You can also sign up for the monthly e-newsletter, take part in monthly competitions and much more!

See you there!

Wildlife Watch

The Wildlife Trusts

# Become a wildflower detective

All detectives need to prepare before they go exploring, and the same is true for wildflower detectives. Before you set out, check these things:

remember to take photos!

- Is the weather forecast good? You don't want to get caught in a thunderstorm!
- Have you got your detectives' equipment ready? See the checklist below for a list of things to take.
- Do you know where you are going and how to find your way back?
- Is an adult coming with you?

## Checklist

| | |
|---|---|
| O pens | O envelopes/plastic bags (to store samples) |
| O pencils | O sun hat |
| O rubber | O sun cream |
| O ruler | O bottle of water |
| O camera | O mobile phone (optional) |
| O magnifying glass | |

## Equipment

Complete the pages in this book with your notes and sketches. Use a ruler to check measurements, and a magnifying glass will give the best view of small plant parts. Take a camera to capture images of entire plants.

grass snake

## Respect wildlife

Keep dogs under control, close gates after you, take your rubbish home, and don't go on to other people's land without asking their permission. You can pick a sample flower, seed or leaf from most plants, but only take what you need and never pull a plant out of the ground or damage it in any way.

**Watch out!**
Stinging and biting creatures like wildflowers too. Make sure your feet and legs are covered and use insect repellent on any bare skin.

# How to use

*Wildflower detectives like to keep records of what they have seen, and you can do that by filling in the pages. There are spaces for your notes, sketches and photographs.*

**Seen it?**
Once you've seen a species, record it by ticking the *Seen It!* stamp.

**Photofile**
Photos of flower species in their natural habitats, plus extra information.

**My observations**
Make notes about your sightings and surroundings.

MY OBSERVATIONS

*What I can see:*

*What I can smell:*

*The weather is:*

These brightly coloured flowers were sometimes scattered over doorsteps in May. They were also used to remove warts and cure colds.

SEEN IT?

MY DRAWINGS AND PHOTOS

212

*I saw this flower in:* *March* O *April* O *May* O

**Drawings:** Use a soft pencil, such as 2B, because the lead is easy to rub out. You don't need to draw the whole plant, just the flower, seed case and leaf shape.

**My drawings and photos**
Fill these spaces with your sketches and photographs.

**Photos:** Concentrate on taking photos of the whole plant and its habitat. You will need plenty of sunlight, but avoid very bright sunshine because it causes strong black shadows. Make sure your shadow is not cast over the plant.

**Pressing flowers:** If a plant is not marked as poisonous or rare, you might like to press some of its petals. Only take petals from plants that are very common or from your garden. Place the petals between two pieces of thick white paper and slide the paper into a large book. Pile heavy books on top, and leave to dry out for about four weeks. Once the petals are dry, you can stick them into this book.

**Main text**
Every right-hand page has a main paragraph to introduce you to each species.

**Close up**
Look here for flower measurements to help you identify each species.

**Colour coding**
The flowers in this book are organized by colour. The species pages are coloured to match, making it easy to find your flower.

**Illustrations**
Detailed artwork shows the key features of each species.

**Fact file**
This box gives you key information about each species.

**Keep safe**
You should not touch any part of species that have this symbol on their pages. Other plants may irritate your skin, so it is wise to wash your hands after touching them.

**Rare and protected**
You must not take any part of plants that have this symbol on their pages because they are endangered, and you could be breaking the law.

**Tick list**
Tick to record when you've seen each species in flower.

## MY OBSERVATIONS

What I can see:

What I can smell:

The weather is:

Bindweed's trumpet-shaped, white or pink flowers open like a fan during the day to attract pollinating insects.

## MY DRAWINGS AND PHOTOS

I saw it flower in: March O April O May O June O

# Bindweed *Convolvulus arvensis*

This plant is easy to recognise due to its large flowers and curling, thin green stems that wrap around other plants. Bindweed is a weed that grows widely, climbing up fences and plants, gradually smothering them. It can also spread by seed and is almost impossible to remove – even a tiny piece of root can grow into a new plant. The roots are fleshy and white, and grow extensively underground.

**TYPE** Bindweed family

**HEIGHT** 50–200 cm

**HABITAT** Widespread, including gardens, roadsides, farmland

**FLOWERS** May to September

**FRUIT** Seeds

**OTHER NAMES** Creeping Jenny, Field bindweed

July O August O September O October O

## MY OBSERVATIONS

What I can see:

What I can smell:

The weather is:

Chamomile often grows as a ground covering plant, and is used to create chamomile lawns, which release their scent when walked on.

## MY DRAWINGS AND PHOTOS

I saw this flower in: March O April O May O June O

# Chamomile *Chamaemelum nobile*

**This daisy-like plant is best known for its delicious scent, which is like a mixture of apples and bubblegum.** Chamomile used to be widespread, but many of its natural habitats have been destroyed. It is now found growing wild in only a few places in the south of England, especially the New Forest.

**TYPE** Daisy family
**HEIGHT** Up to 25 cm
**HABITAT** Short grassland
**FLOWERS** June to August
**FRUIT** Small seeds
**OTHER NAMES** Roman camomile, Ground apple

RARE & PROTECTED

July O August O September O October O

## MY OBSERVATIONS

What I can see:

What I can smell:

The weather is:

Daisies are very common plants. They grow not just in gardens but in grasslands and meadows and also by lakes and ponds.

## MY DRAWINGS AND PHOTOS

I saw it flower in: March O April O May O June O

# Daisy *Bellis perennis*

The tiny white flowers that pepper garden lawns are called daisies and they are often regarded as weeds. The name, daisy, comes from 'day's eye' because the flower opens like an eye when the Sun comes out. Daisies attract pollinating insects, such as bees and hoverflies. Their leaves are hairy and shaped like spoons, and the attractive flowers grow out of the centre of the plant. The plants survive cold and wet winters, and flower from spring onwards. The flowers grow upwards, facing the sun.

**TYPE** Daisy family

**HEIGHT** 2–10 cm

**HABITAT** Widespread in areas of short grass

**FLOWERS** Small white flowers appear all summer

**FRUIT** Tiny seeds, after flowering

**OTHER NAMES** Common daisy, lawn daisy

July O August O September O October O

## MY OBSERVATIONS

What I can see:

What I can smell:

The weather is:

Garlic mustard is an important food plant for orange-tip butterflies. The flowers are pollinated by beetles, flies and bees.

## MY DRAWINGS AND PHOTOS

I saw it flower in: March O April O May O June O

# Garlic mustard *Alliaria petiolata*

A biennial plant, garlic mustard is named after the smell of garlic given off when the leaves are crushed. Each upright stem has clusters of small, snow-white flowers at the top and toothed pale-green leaves spiralling along its length. The leaves are edible – they can be eaten raw in salads or boiled and used as a cooking herb in sauces.

**TYPE** Wild cabbage family

**HEIGHT** Up to 100 cm

**HABITAT** Widespread; thrives in chalky soils

**FLOWERS** Mid-March to May

**FRUIT** Small, black seeds

**OTHER NAMES** Hedge garlic, Jack-by-the-hedge

July ○ August ○ September ○ October ○

## MY OBSERVATIONS

What I can see:

What I can smell:

The weather is:

The blooms of the meadowsweet flower provide food for many insects. Its sweet nectar particularly attracts butterflies and bees.

## MY DRAWINGS AND PHOTOS

I saw this flower in: March O April O May O June O

# Meadowsweet *Filipendula ulmaria*

Meadowsweet has clouds of whitish flowers on tall stems and has a strong perfume. It is popular with flying insects, and thrives in grasslands throughout Britain and Ireland. Long ago, the blooms were scattered over floors to make a house smell sweet.

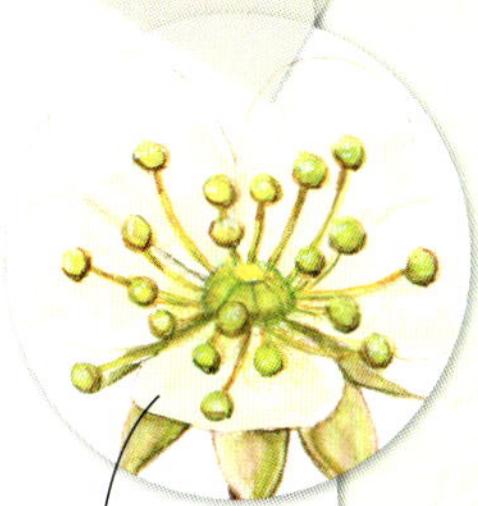

**TYPE** Rose family

**HEIGHT** Up to 125 cm

**HABITAT** Damp meadows, near streams and marshes

**FLOWERS** June to July

**FRUIT** Small, twisted seeds

**OTHER NAMES** Queen of the meadow, Bridewort

July O August O September O October O

## MY OBSERVATIONS

What I can see:

What I can smell:

The weather is:

Fritillary butterflies flock to oxeye daisies in summer. Their wings have orange-brown markings on the upper surfaces, and paler undersides.

SEEN IT?

## MY DRAWINGS AND PHOTOS

I saw this flower in: March O April O May O June O

# Oxeye daisy *Leucanthemum vulgare*

Oxeye daisies are common in meadows, where their bright, bold flower heads catch the eye. They grow from year to year, and spread widely to create a carpet of green, topped with white-and-yellow flower heads. Common daisies look similar to these flowers, but they have smooth, oval leaves and only grow to about 10 cm in height.

flower is 3–5 cm across

**TYPE** Daisy family

**HEIGHT** 10–80 cm

**HABITAT** Grassy places

**FLOWERS** May to September

**FRUIT** Small seeds

**OTHER NAMES** Marguerite, Moon daisy

July O August O September O October O

## MY OBSERVATIONS

What I can see:

What I can smell:

The weather is:

After sea kale has flowered, the seed pods slowly ripen. They dry out and up to 10,000 seeds are released.

## MY DRAWINGS AND PHOTOS

I saw it flower in: March O April O May O June O

# Sea kale *Crambe maritima*

Often found on shingle beaches, sea kale can also survive in the dry, sandy parts of the upper shore. Its thick leaves are able to store water and have a waxy coating on their surface, which stops too much water evaporating. Sea kale rarely flowers before reaching five years of age. This plant used to be steamed and eaten, but it is now rare and should never be picked.

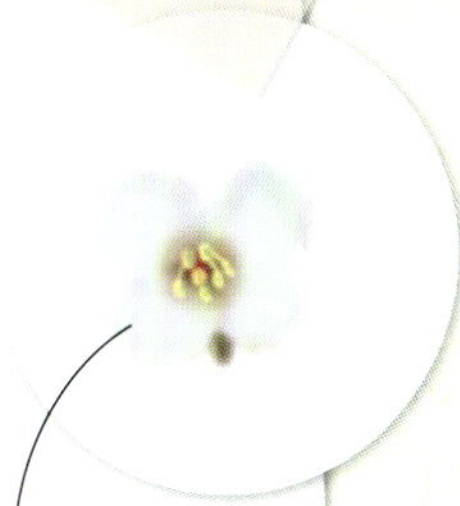

**TYPE** Cabbage family

**HEIGHT** Up to 100 cm

**HABITAT** Upper sandy or shingle shores, pebbly beaches, cliffs

**FLOWERS** White flowers June to August

**FRUIT** Round, green fruits

**OTHER NAMES** Colewort, flowering sea kale

July O August O September O October O

## MY OBSERVATIONS

What I can see:

What I can smell:

The weather is:

Snowdrops often spread out to form beautiful white carpets. They were probably introduced to the UK from central Europe in Medieval times.

## MY DRAWINGS AND PHOTOS

I saw this flower in: December O January O

# Snowdrop *Galanthus nivalis*

Many snowdrops in the countryside have escaped from gardens and become established in the wild. In sheltered places in southwest England, snowdrops may flower as early as Christmas time. Snowdrops flower early in the year using energy stored in underground bulbs. Wild snowdrops have only one flower per stem and have green tips on the inner petal.

**TYPE** Amaryllis family

**HEIGHT** 15–25 cm

**HABITAT** Damp woods, by streams, in meadows

**FLOWERS** Late December to March

**FRUIT** Many small seeds

**OTHER NAMES** Common snowdrop

February O March O

## MY OBSERVATIONS

What I can see:

What I can smell:

The weather is:

Water-plantain makes a good resting spot for dragonflies and damselflies. Its roots provide safe hiding places for small fish, beetles and insect larvae.

SEEN IT?

## MY DRAWINGS AND PHOTOS

I saw this flower in: March O April O May O June O

# Water-plantain *Alisma plantago-aquatica*

You can see the flowers of this plant best in the afternoon, because they are only open between around 1 pm and 7 pm every day. Water-plantain is a stout plant that grows on the edges of watery habitats, especially ponds. It is found everywhere, except northern Scotland.

**TYPE** Water-plantain family

**HEIGHT** Up to 100 cm

**HABITAT** Shallow water, edges of lakes and ponds

**FLOWERS** June to September

**FRUIT** Green, small and nut-like

**OTHER NAMES** Common water-plantain, Mad-dog weed

July ○ August ○ September ○ October ○

## MY OBSERVATIONS

What I can see:

What I can smell:

The weather is:

Wood anemones are found in the same habitats as bluebells, which also come into flower during spring. Look out for them together, as they look beautiful on a woodland floor.

## MY DRAWINGS AND PHOTOS

I saw this flower in: March O April O May O June O

# Wood anemone *Anemone nemorosa*

Wood anemones come into flower in spring, so they decorate woodland floors before many trees have unfurled their leaves. These flowers are able to move towards the light, so they follow the sun as it moves through the sky. Although they have a slight scent, Wood anemones do not contain nectar, so insects visiting the flowers may leave hungry.

**TYPE** Buttercup family
**HEIGHT** Up to 30 cm
**HABITAT** Woodlands, hedgerows and meadows
**FLOWERS** March and April
**FRUIT** Clusters of seeds on old flower head
**OTHER NAMES** Windflower, Thimbleweed

July O August O September O October O

## MY OBSERVATIONS

What I can see:

What I can smell:

The weather is:

Red helleborines usually grow in shady places. These wild flowers are extremely rare, and are found in only a few places in southern England.

SEEN IT?

## MY DRAWINGS AND PHOTOS

I saw this flower in: March O April O May O June O

# Broad-leaved helleborine *Epipactis helleborine*

The Broad-leaved helleborine is a striking plant, with a single spike that grows tall, bearing up to 100 flowers. Its delicately coloured petals are similar to those of other orchids, and are perfectly shaped to put pollen on the back of any visiting bees. Look out for wasps feeding on the nectar, or ants climbing into the cup-shaped flowers.

**TYPE** Orchid family

**HEIGHT** Up to 90 cm

**HABITAT** Woodlands, verges, limestone cliffs

**FLOWERS** July to September

**FRUIT** Pear-shaped

**OTHER NAMES** None

July O August O September O October O

## MY OBSERVATIONS

What I can see:

What I can smell:

The weather is:

If the spathe is cut open the flowers can be seen growing on the spadix. The female flowers are at the base and darker male flowers grow just above them.

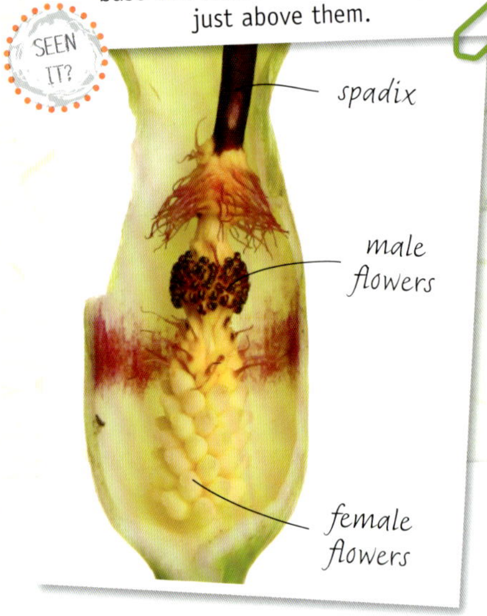


## MY DRAWINGS AND PHOTOS

I saw this flower in: March O April O May O June O

# Lords and ladies *Arum maculatum*

The flowers from a Lords and ladies plant produce a strong, unpleasant smell that attracts insects, which crawl into the flower heads looking for nectar. As they search, the insects rub against the pollen in the male flowers, and fertilise the female ones. Insects may get trapped and die, and their bodies can be seen in the spathe.

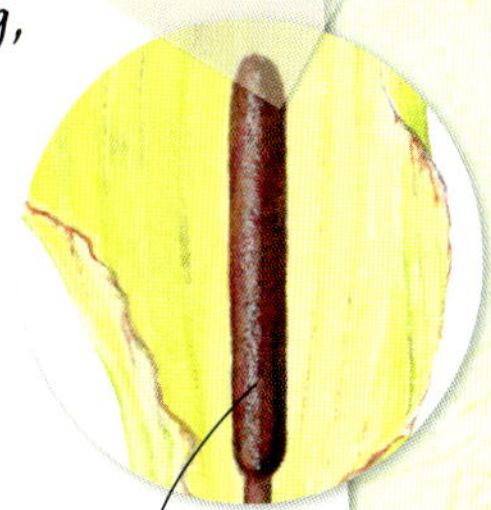

**TYPE** Arum family

**HEIGHT** Up to 50 cm

**HABITAT** Woodlands and hedgerows

**FLOWERS** April and May

**FRUIT** Red berries

**OTHER NAMES** Cuckoo pint, Sweethearts, Adam and Eve, Wild arum

**BEWARE! POISONOUS**

July O August O September O October O

## MY OBSERVATIONS

What I can see:

What I can smell:

The weather is:

The lower petal of this orchid looks like a bee. Male bees are attracted to it, and as they settle on the flower their backs are coated in pollen.

## MY DRAWINGS AND PHOTOS

I saw this flower in: March O April O May O June O

# Bee orchid *Orphrys apifera*

There are around 40 members of the wild orchid family in England and Wales, and Bee orchids are one of the best known and most widespread of them. Each stem holds between two and seven flowers, and each flower looks as if a fat bumblebee has settled on it. Bee orchids are probably extinct in Scotland.

**TYPE** Orchid family

**HEIGHT** Up to 30 cm

**HABITAT** Dry grasslands, especially near chalky or limestone areas

**FLOWERS** June and July

**FRUIT** Long and green with ridges

**OTHER NAMES** None

July O August O September O October O

## MY OBSERVATIONS

What I can see:

What I can smell:

The weather is:

Heathers such as the cross-leaved heath tend to keep their leaves over the winter. Their flowers are usually small and bell-like.

## MY DRAWINGS AND PHOTOS

I saw this flower in: March O April O May O June O

# Cross-leaved heath *Erica tetralix*

This evergreen plant keeps its leaves all year round. They are arranged in a circle, called a whorl, around the stem. Cross-leaved heath has pretty pink flowers, which hang like bells. They stay on the plant until late summer, making a colourful display in boggy places, and attract bees.

**TYPE** Heather family

**HEIGHT** Up to 30 cm

**HABITAT** Wet moors, bogs and heaths

**FLOWERS** July to September

**FRUIT** Small, downy, dark brown capsules

**OTHER NAMES** None

July O August O September O October O

## MY OBSERVATIONS

What I can see:

What I can smell:

The weather is:

Sweet williams, shown here, are related to Deptford pinks, and are popular in gardens. Their flowers are larger than those of Deptford pinks, and grow in a range of colours.

## MY DRAWINGS AND PHOTOS

I saw this flower in: March O April O May O June O

# Deptford pink *Dianthus armeria*

The colour of this flower's petals is often described as cerise, and its stem is greyish. Deptford pinks are biennial, which means that their life-cycle takes two years. This plant produces up to 400 seeds at the end of the summer. A round clump, or rosette, of leaves grows the following year, and flowers bloom the year after that.

**TYPE** Pink family
**HEIGHT** Up to 60 cm
**HABITAT** Dry, grassy areas
**FLOWERS** June to August
**FRUIT** Small capsules
**OTHER NAMES** Mountain pink

RARE & PROTECTED

July O August O September O October O

## MY OBSERVATIONS

What I can see:

What I can smell:

The weather is:

As bees crawl into a Foxglove flower they get covered in pollen. They transfer pollen to other flowers. In doing so they fertilise the ova, which then grow into seeds.

## MY DRAWINGS AND PHOTOS

I saw this flower in: March O April O May O June O

# Foxglove *Digitalis purpurea*

This flower is easy to spot, with its tall spikes that are covered in up to 80 pink flowers. The plant gets its name from the tube-shaped flowers, which are said to resemble little gloves for a fox. The large, pale green leaves are soft on top and woolly underneath.

**TYPE** Digitalis family

**HEIGHT** 40–150 cm

**HABITAT** Woodlands, moors, open spaces, heaths

**FLOWERS** June to August

**FRUIT** Green capsules

**OTHER NAMES** Dead mans' bells, Witches' gloves

**BEWARE! POISONOUS**

July O August O September O October O

## MY OBSERVATIONS

What I can see:

What I can smell:

The weather is:

These flowers are called codlins-and-cream because they are pink and white. Codlins were rosy apples that were boiled in milk and served with cream.

SEEN IT?

## MY DRAWINGS AND PHOTOS

I saw this flower in: March O April O May O June O

# Great willowherb *Epilobium hirsutum*

Willowherbs are unusually tall wildflowers, so it is easy to find them in damp places throughout Britain, except the far north-west, where they rarely grow. They can come from seeds, but they also spread out by fattened roots, called rhizomes, in the soil. This can lead to a large, colourful clump forming in one spot.

**TYPE** Willowherb family

**HEIGHT** Up to 200 cm

**HABITAT** Damp places, such as fens, riverbanks and ditches

**FLOWERS** July and August

**FRUIT** Soft pods contain airborne seeds

**OTHER NAMES** Hairy willowherb, Codlins-and-cream

July O August O September O October O

## MY OBSERVATIONS

What I can see:

What I can smell:

The weather is:

Heather was once used as bedding for animals and bound to make rope, brooms and thatch for roofs. It was even used to repair holes in roads and burnt as a fuel.

SEEN IT?

## MY DRAWINGS AND PHOTOS

I saw this flower in: March O April O May O June O

# Heather *Calluna vulgaris*

You can find Heather in both damp and dry places. It grows into bushes with many branches and each bush can reach 100 cm tall and 100 cm wide. It is most likely to grow in acid soil conditions. Heather keeps its leaves over the winter, and its flowers, which are sometimes white, can last from spring to autumn.

**TYPE** Heather family

**HEIGHT** 50–100 cm

**HABITAT** Heaths, moors, bogs, open spaces and woods

**FLOWERS** July to September

**FRUIT** Capsules

**OTHER NAMES** Common heather, Ling

July O August O September O October O

## MY OBSERVATIONS

What I can see:

What I can smell:

The weather is:

Herb-robert turns red in the autumn. Although it is very pretty, this plant can quickly take over an area, killing off weaker plants that cannot reach the light.

## MY DRAWINGS AND PHOTOS

I saw this flower in: March O April O May O June O

# Herb-robert *Geranium robertianum*

Herb-robert is a survivor. It can live in sun or shade, and can cope with mild winter weather, unlike many other wildflowers that die down after the summer. As Herb-robert is not fussy about the type of soil it lives in, it is common throughout Britain.

**TYPE** Crane's-bill family
**HEIGHT** 10–50 cm
**HABITAT** Hedgerows, near shady walls, pathways, woods
**FLOWERS** April to October
**FRUIT** Long and hairy
**OTHER NAMES** Red robin, Stinky-Bob

July O August O September O October O

# MY OBSERVATIONS

What I can see:

What I can smell:

The weather is:

In some places, Indian balsam is called 'bee-bums', because when a bee is exploring inside the flower, feeding on nectar, all you can see is its tail end!

SEEN IT?

# MY DRAWINGS AND PHOTOS

I saw this flower in: March O April O May O June O

# Indian balsam *Impatiens glandulifera*

Indian balsam was introduced to Britain in 1839, having been brought from the Himalayan mountain region. It is one of the tallest wildflowers, and is seen all over Britain, especially in England and Wales. It is sometimes thought of as a pest. The flowers produce lots of nectar, so there are likely to be bees, wasps and other insects nearby.

**TYPE** Often treated as a weed

**HEIGHT** 100–200 cm

**HABITAT** Wet places, near rivers and streams

**FLOWERS** July to October

**FRUIT** Explosive seed pods

**OTHER NAMES** Policeman's balsam, Kiss-me-on-the-mountain

July O August O September O October O

## MY OBSERVATIONS

What I can see:

What I can smell:

The weather is:

Clumps of purple loosestrife attract many types of wildlife, including bumblebees, honeybees, brimstone butterflies and elephant hawk-moths.

## MY DRAWINGS AND PHOTOS

I saw this flower in: March O April O May O June O

# Purple loosestrife *Lythrum salicaria*

*Purple loosestrife plants often grow close together in wet places, with their magenta-pink flower spikes standing tall above the green leaves.* These plants are perennial, which means they can live for more than two years before dying down, and the flowers last for the whole summer.

**TYPE** Wetland plant that grows in groups

**HEIGHT** Up to 200 cm

**HABITAT** Wetlands, near pond edges, marshes and fens

**FLOWERS** June to August

**FRUIT** Capsule containing tiny seeds

**OTHER NAMES** None

July O August O September O October O

## MY OBSERVATIONS

What I can see:

What I can smell:

The weather is:

Red campion blooms as bluebells are finishing. Woodlands with wood anemones, bluebells and red campion go through shades of white, blue and pink from spring to autumn.

SEEN IT?

## MY DRAWINGS AND PHOTOS

I saw this flower in: March O April O May O June O

# Red campion *Silene dioica*

The flowers of red campion are mostly pink rather than red. There are five petals on each flower head, but it can look as if there are more when the petals are very deeply lobed. The flowers are visited by bumblebees, butterflies and moths, which feed on the sweet nectar.

**TYPE** Pink family

**HEIGHT** Up to 100 cm

**HABITAT** Hedgerows, paths, grassy places

**FLOWERS** March to October

**FRUIT** Round, dry capsule

**OTHER NAMES** Adders' flower, Jack-by-the-hedge, Scalded apples

July O August O September O October O

## MY OBSERVATIONS

What I can see:

What I can smell:

The weather is:

According to folklore, if you have thrift in your garden you will never be poor. Named after the practice of taking care of your money, it was depicted on the back of an old English coin.

SEEN IT?

## MY DRAWINGS AND PHOTOS

I saw this flower in: March O April O May O June O

# Thrift *Armeria maritima*

Thrift has candyfloss flower heads growing above a dense mat of leaves. It is an unusual plant that can grow in very dry places, especially at the coast. The clump of leaves makes a safe home for beetles and other insects, and bees visit the pink flowers. When many clumps grow together, they create a cushion of soft leaves.

**TYPE** Thrift family

**HEIGHT** Up to 20 cm

**HABITAT** Rocky places, near coasts, cliffs, marshes

**FLOWERS** April to October

**FRUIT** Capsules

**OTHER NAMES** Sea thrift, Sea pink, Sea cushion

July ○ August ○ September ○ October ○

## MY OBSERVATIONS

What I can see:

What I can smell:

The weather is:

Although the flower of this plant is very distinctive, you can still recognise it when it is not in bloom by its large, toothed leaves, which are mostly divided into five leaflets.

SEEN IT?

## MY DRAWINGS AND PHOTOS

I saw this flower in: March O April O May O June O

# Marsh cinquefoil *Potentilla palustris*

The deep pink or red flowers of the Marsh cinquefoil are unlike any other flower. They are star shaped, and grow at the top of upright magenta-coloured stems. There are five sepals and smaller purple petals form a layer on top of them. Other cinquefoils, which grow in dry places, have yellow flowers and are not star shaped.

**TYPE** Rose family

**HEIGHT** 20–50 cm

**HABITAT** Wet places, fens, marshes, bogs and near ponds

**FLOWERS** June and July

**FRUIT** Dry, small and papery

**OTHER NAMES** Swamp cinquefoil

July O August O September O October O

## MY OBSERVATIONS

What I can see:

What I can smell:

The weather is:

This flower is rare, as each plant only produces a few heavy seeds that are not easily transported to new areas. It has also been killed off in many areas by the use of chemicals.

## MY DRAWINGS AND PHOTOS

I saw this flower in: March O April O May O June O

# Pheasant's eye *Adonis annua*

Pheasant's eye is a type of buttercup, with five to eight glossy scarlet petals and feathery leaves. By August the flowers are dying down to be replaced by large seed cases. When the seeds fall to the ground they may rest there – they are described as 'dormant' – until the following spring, or even several years later.

**TYPE** Buttercup family
**HEIGHT** Up to 40 cm
**HABITAT** Farmers' fields
**FLOWERS** June to August
**FRUIT** Large and wrinkled
**OTHER NAMES** Blood drops, Jack in the green, Rose-a-ruby

RARE & PROTECTED

July O August O September O October O

## MY OBSERVATIONS

What I can see:

What I can smell:

The weather is:

Poppies are common in farmers' fields because they grow particularly well on soil that has been disturbed, and they can flower and seed themselves before the farmer's crop is harvested.

## MY DRAWINGS AND PHOTOS

I saw this flower in: March O April O May O June O

# Poppy *Papaver rhoeas*

The scarlet, papery petals of the Poppy are often black at the base. The flowers grow at the top of a long, hairy stalk and each petal is black at the base. The leaves are distinctive, with their feathery appearance and toothed edges.

**TYPE** Poppy family

**HEIGHT** 40–80 cm

**HABITAT** Fields, wasteland, roadsides

**FLOWERS** June to August

**FRUIT** Round capsule

**OTHER NAMES** Common poppy, Flanders poppy, Corn poppy

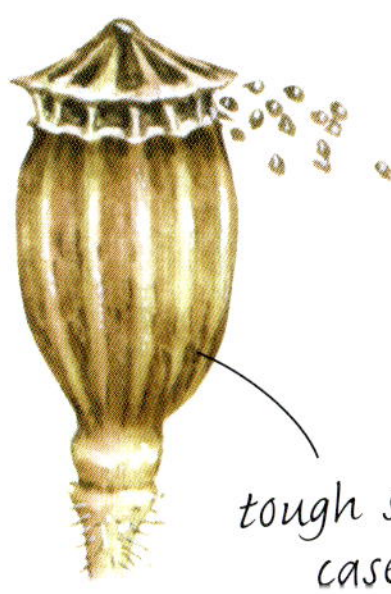


July O August O September O October O

## MY OBSERVATIONS

What I can see:

What I can smell:

The weather is:

The petals of scarlet pimpernel close when air pressure drops – a sign that rain might be due. It can also be used to tell the time, as petals open in the morning and close mid-afternoon.

## MY DRAWINGS AND PHOTOS

I saw this flower in: March O April O May O June O

# Scarlet pimpernel *Anagalis arvensis*

*It is easy to overlook the tiny red flowers of the Scarlet pimpernel. These plants are small and grow low to the ground, with the stems sprawling out along the soil. Purple hairs inside the flower attract many insects in summer. Scarlet pimpernels are common throughout Britain, but are mostly found near the coast in Scotland.*

**TYPE** Primrose family

**HEIGHT** Up to 20 cm

**HABITAT** Farms, grassland, open areas and sand dunes

**FLOWERS** May to September

**FRUIT** Tiny brown capsules

**OTHER NAMES** Red chickweed, Red pimpernel, Shepherd's clock

*July* O *August* O *September* O *October* O

# MY OBSERVATIONS

What I can see:

What I can smell:

The weather is:

Beautiful bluebells carpet woodland floors in spring, creating a stunning sight. Visitors like to enjoy the floral display and strong fragrance.

# MY DRAWINGS AND PHOTOS

I saw this flower in: March O April O May O June O

# Bluebell *Hyacinthoides non-scripta*

**These plants normally bear blue flowers, but there are violet, pink and white ones too.** Bluebells were once common, but many bluebell woods have been damaged by people picking the flowers and digging up the bulbs. A variant species called the Spanish bluebell is also a threat – it can cross pollinate with the English variety to create a hybrid.

**TYPE** Lily family

**HEIGHT** 10–40 cm

**HABITAT** Woodlands and coastal cliffs

**FLOWERS** April to June

**FRUIT** Capsules

**OTHER NAMES** Wood bells, Auld man's bell, Jacinth, Ring o' bells

RARE & PROTECTED

July O August O September O October O

## MY OBSERVATIONS

What I can see:

What I can smell:

The weather is:

Brooklime grows in wet ground and in water. Its leaves and stems provide shelter for small pond-living animals such as insects, sticklebacks (small fish) and tadpoles.

SEEN IT?

## MY DRAWINGS AND PHOTOS

I saw this flower in: March O April O May O June O

# Brooklime *Veronica beccabunga*

**Brooklime is a creeping plant that produces stems that grow along the ground.** Roots grow from these stems at places called nodes. The flowering stems grow upright and produce star-shaped blooms throughout the summer. The petals are usually blue, but pink ones grow too, and there is a white 'eye' in the centre of each bloom.

**TYPE** Water plant of the Speedwell family

**HEIGHT** Up to 30 cm

**HABITAT** Any damp ground, often grows in shallow water

**FLOWERS** May to September

**FRUIT** Round flat capsules

**OTHER NAMES** Water pimpernel, Cow cress, Limewort

July O August O September O October O

## MY OBSERVATIONS

What I can see:

What I can smell:

The weather is:

## MY DRAWINGS AND PHOTOS

This plant grows throughout Britain. In some places it is called carpenter's herb, because it was once used to stop bleeding and people often grew it in their gardens for that purpose.

SEEN IT?

I saw this flower in: March O April O May O June O

# Bugle *Ajuga reptans*

Bugle forms dense mats of green leaves, covering the ground. Flower stems grow upwards and bear clusters of many small, purple flowers. Occasionally, the flowers are pink or white. Bugle leaves are unusual because they have a dark green background colour, with a purple sheen. Butterflies often flitter around this plant and feed on it.

**TYPE** Dead-nettle family

**HEIGHT** Up to 20 cm

**HABITAT** Any damp ground, often grows in shallow water

**FLOWERS** April to June

**FRUIT** Nutlets

**OTHER NAMES** Blue bugle, Bugleweed, Carpetweed, Bugleherb

July O August O September O October O

## MY OBSERVATIONS

What I can see:

What I can smell:

The weather is:

Butterworts are pretty insect-eaters. Flowers grow from single stems, which emerge out of a single rosette of leaves at ground level.

SEEN IT?

## MY DRAWINGS AND PHOTOS

I saw this flower in: March O April O May O June O

# Butterwort *Pinguicula vulgaris*

These violet flowers attract bees, to pollinate them. A sticky leaf attracts flies and other small insects, holding them like glue and stopping them from breathing. The leaves then curl around the bugs and produce chemicals that start to dissolve their bodies. This releases nutrients that help the plant to grow.

**TYPE** Fly-eating plant
**HEIGHT** Up to 15 cm
**HABITAT** Bogs and other damp places
**FLOWERS** May to August
**FRUIT** Tough, oval-shaped capsule
**OTHER NAMES** None

July ○ August ○ September ○ October ○

## MY OBSERVATIONS

What I can see:

What I can smell:

The weather is:

Columbine is poisonous but it was once used to treat digestive problems, and as a painkiller. It was also thought that carrying a posy of columbine would make people fall in love.

## MY DRAWINGS AND PHOTOS

I saw this flower in: March O April O May O June O

# Columbine *Aquilegia vulgaris*

***Columbine flowers grow on tall stems.*** The central part of the flower is made up of five petals, and a rosette of coloured leaves surrounds them, to create a drooping, stunning bloom. Wild columbines are deep blue to purple in colour and have a fragrance.

**TYPE** Buttercup family

**HEIGHT** Up to 100 cm

**HABITAT** Open woods, fens and grasslands

**FLOWERS** May to August

**FRUIT** Small and dry but with many seeds

**OTHER NAMES** None

BEWARE! POISONOUS

July O August O September O October O

## MY OBSERVATIONS

What I can see:

What I can smell:

The weather is:

Cornflowers were used in herbal medicine to treat eye problems, and young men in love often wore them in their buttonholes.

SEEN IT?

## MY DRAWINGS AND PHOTOS

I saw this flower in: March O April O May O June O

# Cornflower *Centaurea cyanus*

Cornflower blooms are such a brilliant blue that they have given their name to a shade of the colour. Each bloom is actually a collection of tiny flowers, called florets. The outer florets are blue to purple, and the inner florets are slightly redder. Cornflowers were once common in farmers' fields, but are now a rare sight.

**TYPE** Daisy family

**HEIGHT** 40–90 cm

**HABITAT** Fields

**FLOWERS** June to August

**FRUIT** Small

**OTHER NAMES** Bachelor's button, Bluebottle, Basketflower

RARE & PROTECTED

July O August O September O October O

## MY OBSERVATIONS

What I can see:

What I can smell:

The weather is:

Insects, such as this butterfly, are attracted to these flowers because they suck the sugary nectar that the flowers produce. In return, the insects pollinate the plants.

## MY DRAWINGS AND PHOTOS

I saw this flower in: March O April O May O June O

# Devil's-bit scabious *Succisa pratensis*

**The round bloom of a Devil's-bit scabious is not one flower, but many little florets all clustered together.** The petals are usually purple-blue, but are sometimes pinkish. The tiny anthers in each flower poke out above the petals. Bumblebees are drawn to the flowers because they prefer purple blooms to those of any other colour.

**TYPE** Teasel family

**HEIGHT** 10–75 cm

**HABITAT** Damp grasslands, open areas, hedgerows, mountain slopes

**FLOWERS** June to September

**FRUIT** Dry and papery

**OTHER NAMES** Pincushion flowers

July ○ August ○ September ○ October ○

## MY OBSERVATIONS

What I can see:

What I can smell:

The weather is:

Harebells can live from year to year because they grow rhizomes. In the autumn, the plants die down but the rhizomes are safe in the ground, and produce new stems in the spring.

## MY DRAWINGS AND PHOTOS

I saw this flower in: March O April O May O June O

# Harebell *Campanula rotundifolia*

The flowers of the harebell are delicate and swing when a breeze catches them. Each stem may bear just one flower, or several growing on a spike. The leaves grow long and thin near the flowers, but round when they are near the base. At ground level, creeping stems become thick and store food over winter for the plant.

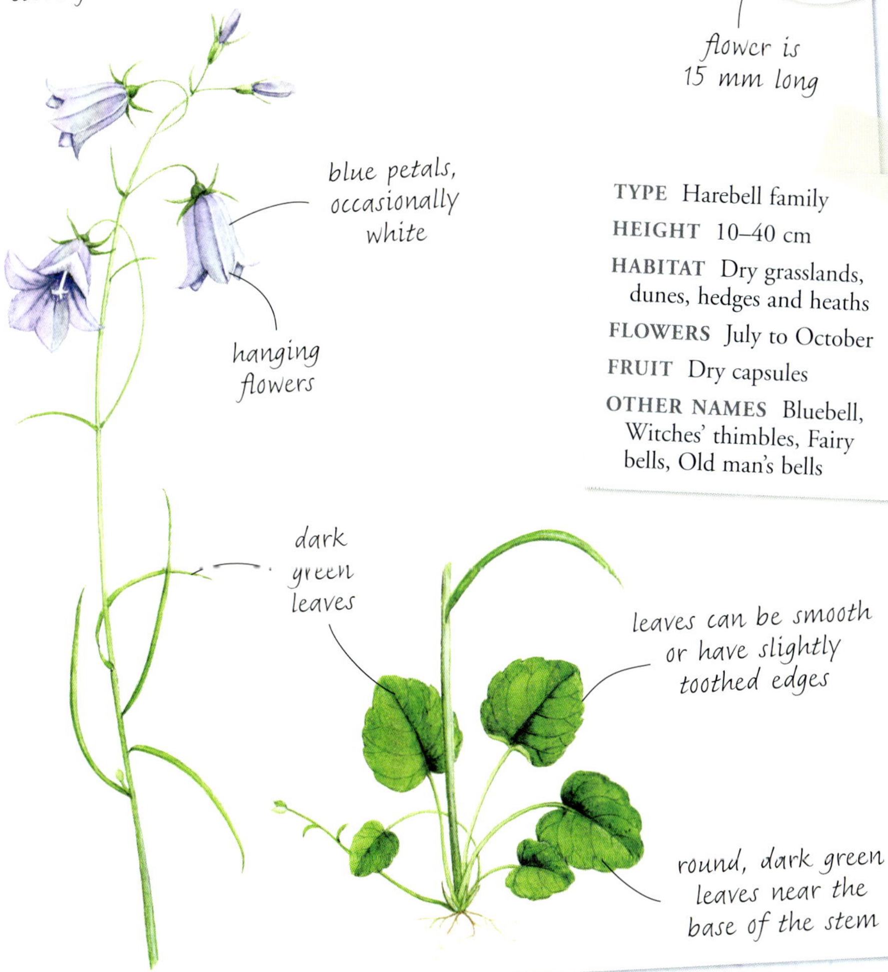


**TYPE** Harebell family

**HEIGHT** 10–40 cm

**HABITAT** Dry grasslands, dunes, hedges and heaths

**FLOWERS** July to October

**FRUIT** Dry capsules

**OTHER NAMES** Bluebell, Witches' thimbles, Fairy bells, Old man's bells

July O August O September O October O

## MY OBSERVATIONS

What I can see:

What I can smell:

The weather is:

Wild pansies are also part of the violet family and they grow in dry grasslands and gardens. Their flowers can be violet, yellow or a combination of the two.

## MY DRAWINGS AND PHOTOS

I saw this flower in: March O April O May O June O

# Marsh violet *Viola palustris*

**Violets look like pansies, but are a little smaller.** Marsh violet flowers are pale lilac or violet in colour and the lower petal has deep purple veins. After the flower dies the petals fall off, but the five sepals stay attached to the stalk and the growing seed capsule. The caterpillars of fritillary butterflies use this as a food plant.

**TYPE** Violet family

**HEIGHT** 5–20 cm

**HABITAT** Bogs, marshes, riverbanks and damp meadows

**FLOWERS** April to July

**FRUIT** Egg-shaped

**OTHER NAMES** Alpine marsh violet

July ○ August ○ September ○ October ○

# MY OBSERVATIONS

What I can see:

What I can smell:

The weather is:

Cranesbills are also called geraniums. They can survive from year to year, and grow in bigger and bigger mounds. Most geraniums are blue, violet, purple or pink.

# MY DRAWINGS AND PHOTOS

I saw this flower in: March O April O May O June O

# Meadow cranesbill *Geranium pratense*

The purple-blue flowers of the Meadow cranesbill grow tall above the surface of a clump of dark green leaves, providing a summer splash of colour. These flowers grow all over Britain but look similar to Wood cranesbill, which is paler in colour, but is only found in the north of England and Scotland.

**TYPE** Cranesbill family
**HEIGHT** 20–80 cm
**HABITAT** Meadows, woods, grasslands, dunes and roadsides
**FLOWERS** June to September
**FRUIT** Small but with a long 'beak'
**OTHER NAMES** None

July O August O September O October O

## MY OBSERVATIONS

What I can see:

What I can smell:

The weather is:

Long-tongued bees are attracted to the pink flowers of the sea pea plant, and pollinate them. Pigeons and doves eat the pea-sized seeds.

SEEN IT?

## MY DRAWINGS AND PHOTOS

I saw this flower in: March O April O May O June O

# Sea pea *Lathyrus japonicus*

Pretty sea pea plants provide colour to dry areas of shingle beaches. Their delicate leaves and tendrils spread out in clumps up to 2 metres wide. Sea peas rarely flower before their third summer. The pea-like seeds are carried by seawater to new areas, and can survive for up to five years before they start to grow into new plants.

**TYPE** Pea family

**HEIGHT** Up to 20 cm

**HABITAT** Upper shore, dry shingle, sandy banks

**FLOWERS** Pink/purple flowers from May to August

**FRUIT** Pods containing seeds

**OTHER NAMES** Beach pea

RARE & PROTECTED

July O August O September O October O

## MY OBSERVATIONS

What I can see:

What I can smell:

The weather is:

Teasels are especially popular with goldfinches. These bold, noisy, colourful birds flock to the dry heads to feast on the seeds inside. A group of goldfinches is called a charm.

SEEN IT?

## MY DRAWINGS AND PHOTOS

I saw this flower in: March O April O May O June O

# Teasel *Dipascus fullonum*

Teasel plants produce flowers only in their second year. In the first year, the plant grows a large rosette of leaves at ground level. In the second year, a large stem grows from the rosette to hold the flower head. The rosette then dies back and paired prickly leaves grow on the flower stem.

**TYPE** Teasel family

**HEIGHT** Up to 200 cm

**HABITAT** Grasslands, near streams, roadsides, wasteland and by railways

**FLOWERS** July and August

**FRUIT** Dry flower heads hold many dry fruits

**OTHER NAMES** Wild teasel, Brushes-and-combs

July O August O September O October O

## MY OBSERVATIONS

What I can see:

What I can smell:

The weather is:

Tufted vetch is also known as cow vetch because it can be fed to cattle. It grows in wild woodlands where deer may roam. Like other pea plants, it adds goodness to the soil.

SEEN IT?

## MY DRAWINGS AND PHOTOS

I saw this flower in: March O April O May O June O

# Tufted vetch *Vicia cracca*

Like other members of the pea family, tufted vetch has many oval leaflets that are paired on one stalk. Curling tendrils grow from the end of some leaflets. They help pea plants to climb and clamber high, catching the sun and blocking the light from other plants. The blue-purple flowers grow in clusters where leaflets connect to the stem.

**TYPE** Pea family

**HEIGHT** 30–200 cm

**HABITAT** Grassy places, hedgerows, bushes and ditches

**FLOWERS** June to August

**FRUIT** Bright green pods

**OTHER NAMES** Cow vetch

July ○ August ○ September ○ October ○

## MY OBSERVATIONS

What I can see:

What I can smell:

The weather is:

Cowslips have long been used in traditional medicine to treat headaches and coughs. The plant can also be made into wine, but as it is becoming rare it shouldn't be picked.

SEEN IT?

## MY DRAWINGS AND PHOTOS

I saw this flower in: March O April O May O June O

# Cowslip *Primula veris*

Cowslips have rosettes of large, wrinkled leaves at the base and clusters of yellow flowers that are held high on tall stems. They were once widespread, but became less common in recent years. Today, hedgerows and meadows are often left uncut until autumn, so flowers like these have a better chance of surviving.

**TYPE** Primrose family

**HEIGHT** 10–30 cm

**HABITAT** Grassy places, open woods, meadows and roadsides

**FLOWERS** April and May

**FRUIT** Capsules

**OTHER NAMES** Herb-Peter

July O August O September O October O

## MY OBSERVATIONS

What I can see:

What I can smell:

The weather is:

Dandelion seeds are easily carried by the wind to new areas where they settle and germinate – creating fields full of dandelions.

## MY DRAWINGS AND PHOTOS

I saw this flower in: March ○ April ○ May ○ June ○

# Dandelion *Taraxacum officinale*

One of the most common flowering plants, dandelions get their name from the old French name for the plant, 'dent de lion'. This means 'tooth' of the lion because the leaf edges look like a row of sharp teeth. They are considered weeds by many gardeners, but their bright-yellow flowers are a favourite of many pollinating insects. Other types of wildlife, such as rabbits, enjoy eating both flowers and leaves.

**TYPE** Asteraceae family

**HEIGHT** 5–74 cm

**HABITAT** Gardens, parks and woodlands

**FLOWERS** Yellow, from March to October

**FRUIT** Tiny seeds with fluffy hairs, from summer to autumn

**OTHER NAMES** Common dandelion

July O August O September O October O

## MY OBSERVATIONS

What I can see:

What I can smell:

The weather is:

More common St John's wort plants are similar to the flax-leaved type, but they mostly have more obvious anthers and can grow to a height of 100 cm.

## MY DRAWINGS AND PHOTOS

I saw this flower in: March O April O May O June O

# Flax-leaved St John's wort *Hypericum linarifolium*

Flax-leaved St John's worts have golden yellow flowers. After the flowers die down the seed capsules split, releasing up to 250 tiny seeds that are carried by the wind. This plant is very rare in Britain, and is only found in parts of North Wales and on Dartmoor in Southwest England, and a few other scattered locations.

**TYPE** St John's wort family
**HEIGHT** Up to 30 cm
**HABITAT** Rocky ground and near cliffs
**FLOWERS** June and July
**FRUIT** Brown capsule
**OTHER NAMES** None

RARE & PROTECTED

July O August O September O October O

## MY OBSERVATIONS

What I can see:

What I can smell:

The weather is:

Lesser celandine is one of the first wildflowers to bloom. It provides food for insects, especially hungry bumblebees that have just come out of hibernation.

## MY DRAWINGS AND PHOTOS

I saw this flower in: March O April O May O June O

# Lesser celandine *Ranunculus ficaria*

Lesser celandine is a brief visitor to woodlands and other natural habitats. It grows as a patch of rosettes on the ground, topped by bright yellow flowers. However, it dies back once flowering has finished. The flowers contain between eight and 12 little petals, which only open when the sun is shining.

**TYPE** Buttercup family

**HEIGHT** 2–20 cm

**HABITAT** Damp woodlands and meadows, near hedgerows and by streams

**FLOWERS** March to May

**FRUIT** Rounded seed heads

**OTHER NAMES** Pilewort, Spring messenger

BEWARE! POISONOUS

July ○ August ○ September ○ October ○

## MY OBSERVATIONS

What I can see:

What I can smell:

The weather is:

These brightly coloured flowers were sometimes scattered over doorsteps in May. They were also used to remove warts and cure colds.

SEEN IT?

## MY DRAWINGS AND PHOTOS

I saw this flower in: March O April O May O June O

# Marsh marigold *Caltha palustris*

Marsh marigolds can form large clumps of deep green, shiny leaves, topped by bright golden flowers. The plants are tough and can survive in shady or sunny places, but they prefer damp soil. Marsh marigolds used to be common, but many of their marsh and bog habitats have been lost.

**TYPE** Buttercup family

**HEIGHT** 20–30 cm

**HABITAT** Marshes, wet meadows and damp woods

**FLOWERS** March to July

**FRUIT** Capsules

**OTHER NAMES** Kingcup, Mayflower, Water-bubbles

BEWARE! POISONOUS

RARE & PROTECTED

July O August O September O October O

## MY OBSERVATIONS

What I can see:

What I can smell:

The weather is:

The base of each primrose petal is an orange-yellow, giving a golden centre to each flower. Many flowers grow, topping slender stalks that emerge from a central rosette of leaves.

SEEN IT?

## MY DRAWINGS AND PHOTOS

I saw this flower in: March O April O May O June O

# Primrose *Primula vulgaris*

The yellow petals of the primrose are as pale as butter, but they turn orange near their bases. Primrose's Latin name – Primula – comes from the Latin for 'first little one' and 'primrose' means 'first rose'. This is one of the early spring flowering plants that bloom when there are few other flowers around.

**TYPE** Primrose family

**HEIGHT** 10–30 cm

**HABITAT** Hedgerows, grassy places, woods, mountains and cliffs

**FLOWERS** March to June

**FRUIT** Capsules

**OTHER NAMES** Butter rose, Common primrose

July O August O September O October O

## MY OBSERVATIONS

What I can see:

What I can smell:

The weather is:

Silverweed appears in many old stories and folklore. It was regarded as a useful plant, and its leaves were even put in shoes to keep feet dry!

## MY DRAWINGS AND PHOTOS

I saw this flower in: March O April O May O June O

# Silverweed *Potentilla anserina*

This is a creeping plant that spreads out on bare soils. The feathery leaves are divided up into many pairs of leaflets that are covered in fine, silvery hairs. Long creeping stems, called stolons, grow on the ground beneath the leaves and flowers. Silverweed has been used in herbal remedies, and its roots were used to make tea.

**TYPE** Rose family
**HEIGHT** 5–20 cm
**HABITAT** Wasteland, damp grassy places
**FLOWERS** May to August
**FRUIT** Dry and papery
**OTHER NAMES** Cinquefoil

July O August O September O October O

## MY OBSERVATIONS

What I can see:

What I can smell:

The weather is:

Sunflower seeds in the flower's centre are oval with black-and-cream stripes. They are the favourite foods of mice and some birds.

## MY DRAWINGS AND PHOTOS

I saw this flower in: March O April O May O June O

# Sunflower *Helianthus*

These tall, flowering plants grow as a single stem with a huge flowerhead. They are not native to the UK but are sometimes seen in field margins where they are allowed to grow to provide food for farmland birds. Some farmers even grow fields of sunflowers as crops, harvesting the seeds for wild bird food mixes. Sunflowers are also a favourite with gardeners and are grown for their striking appearance.

**TYPE** Daisy family

**HEIGHT** Up to 300 cm

**HABITAT** Farmland and gardens

**FLOWERS** Large yellow flowers with black or golden centres, from mid to late summer

**FRUIT** Medium-sized seeds, after flowering

**OTHER NAMES** Common sunflower

*July* O *August* O *September* O *October* O

## MY OBSERVATIONS

What I can see:

What I can smell:

The weather is:

Ducks, fish and insects can hide amongst iris plants. Yellow irises remove dirt from water, and are used in sewage farms.

## MY DRAWINGS AND PHOTOS

I saw this flower in: March ○ April ○ May ○ June ○

# Yellow iris *Iris Pseudocorus*

Irises grow in wet places, and may even have their roots in water. They can spread by means of seeds, but also spread by rhizomes, which are swollen roots that produce buds in spring. When they spread by rhizomes, irises can quickly grow into large clumps and create a perfect habitat for pond wildlife.

**TYPE** Grow from rhizomes

**HEIGHT** Up to 100 cm

**HABITAT** Wet places such as meadows, ditches, marshes and near rivers or streams

**FLOWERS** June to August

**FRUIT** Three-sided and long

**OTHER NAMES** Yellow flag

July O August O September O October O

## MY OBSERVATIONS

What I can see:

What I can smell:

The weather is:

The stems of yellow rattle have unusual black marks on them, which helps to identify this wildflower. The yellow flowers are small, and protected by green bracts.

SEEN IT?

## MY DRAWINGS AND PHOTOS

I saw this flower in: March ○ April ○ May ○ June ○

# Yellow rattle *Rhinanthus minor*

**Yellow rattle steals nutrients from its neighbouring plants.** It stops grass from growing, which helps other types of wild plant to survive in meadows. At the end of the summer the seed capsules ripen and seeds inside become loose. When the capsule is shaken, the seeds rattle around, which is how the plant got its name.

**TYPE** Figwort family
**HEIGHT** 20–40 cm
**HABITAT** Open grassy places
**FLOWERS** June to September
**FRUIT** Dry capsules with seeds that rattle
**OTHER NAMES** Cockscomb

July O  August O  September O  October O

# Glossary

**Annual** A plant that takes one year to complete its life cycle.

**Berry** A small, soft fruit with small seeds.

**Biennial** A plant that takes two years to complete its life cycle

**Bloom** When the flowers open.

**Bract** A leaf-like part of a plant, found underneath a flower or its stalk.

**Bud** A rounded, undeveloped leaf or flower, often at the end of a twig or shoot.

**Bulb** A swollen part of the plant that grows under the ground, or at ground level. It contains the beginnings of the next year's stems and leaves.

**Catkin** A long, often hanging cluster of tiny flowers, on trees such as willows, oaks and birches.

**Compound (leaf shape)** Made up of several smaller leaves called leaflets.

**Coppice** To cut back the stems of a tree to near ground level, causing many long, new shoots to grow up.

**Cultivate** To grow especially.

**Deciduous** Trees that drop their leaves every autumn.

**Evergreen** Trees that keep their leaves all year round.

**Floret** A small flower that is part of a bigger flower head.

**Fruit** The hard, soft or fleshy covering of the seed of flowering plants and trees.

**Germinate** To start to grow.

**Girth** The measurement around something, such as a tree trunk.

**Hand (leaf shape)** Multiple lobes that spread out like fingers.

**Hybrid** A tree that is the offspring of two similar tree species eg the common lime.

**Larva** The worm-like young of an insect, e.g. a caterpillar, that changes into a winged, flying adult.

**Leaflet** A leaf or leaf-like section of a compound leaf.

**Lobe** A rounded part of a leaf that sticks out.

**Long (leaf shape)** Slender and elongated.

**Native** Originally from a particular country.

**Needle (leaf shape)** Slender and pointed, like a needle.

**Node** The place where a leaf grows out from a stem.

**Oval (leaf shape)** Rounded, with a tapering point.

**Perennial** A plant that lives for more than two years.

**Pollard** To cut back the top branches of a tree to encourage more to grow.

**Pollen** A powder made my flowers. It is carried to other flowers so they produce new seeds.

**Raceme** A hanging group of flowers.

**Rhizome** A thickened stem that grows underground or at ground level.

**Rosette** The way leaves are arranged around a stem at ground level.

**Scrubland** An area of land, often covered with shrubs, bushes and grassland.

**Seed** A small fruit produced from a plant. New plants grow from seeds.

**Sepal** One of the small leaves under the flower.

**Shoot** A new growth of a plant.

**Spadix** A flower spike.

**Spathe** A thick leaf that protects the growing flower.

**Stalk** The long, narrow part of a plant that supports the leaves, flowers and fruit, and carries water and nutrients up them.

**Stamen** The male part of a flower that makes pollen.

**Stigma** One of the female parts of a flower.

**Style** One of the female parts of a flower.

**Tendril** A thin growth that wraps itself around things.